AMERICA'S BEST
BARBECUE

AMERICA'S BEST
BARBECUE

Recipes and Techniques for Prize-Winning Ribs, Wings, Brisket, and More

ARTHUR AGUIRRE

Skyhorse Publishing

Skyhorse Publishing books may be purchased in bulk at special discounts for sales promotion, corporate gifts, fund-raising, or educational purposes. Special editions can also be created to specifications. For details, contact the Special Sales Department, Skyhorse Publishing, 307 West 36th Street, 11th Floor, New York, NY 10018 or info@skyhorsepublishing.com.

Skyhorse and Skyhorse Publishing are registered trademarks of Skyhorse Publishing, Inc., a Delaware corporation.

Visit our website at www.skyhorsepublishing.com.

10 9 8 7 6 5 4 3 2 1

Library of Congress Cataloging-in-Publication Data

Aguirre, Arthur.
America's best barbecue : recipes and techniques for prize-winning ribs, wings, brisket, and more / Arthur Aguirre.
 pages cm
 ISBN 978-1-62636-256-7 (alk. paper)
1. Barbecuing–United States. 2. Cooking (Smoked foods) 3. Barbecuing–Competitions–United States. I. Title. II. Title: Recipes and techniques for prize-winning ribs, wings, brisket, and more. III. Title: America's best barbeque.
TX840.B3A339 2013
641.7'6–dc23
                                2013031766

Printed in China

CONTENTS

INTRODUCTION

BBQ.I.AM

As if I needed to write a cookbook to show how passionate I am about barbecue. My devotion for smoked hunks of meat culled from heritage cattle, hogs, and fowl was an evolution that started a decade ago. It began the day I realized that I had no idea what barbecue was or how to prepare such smoky goodness. This epiphany came after I served undercooked pieces of chicken to my friends at a backyard gathering.

Not to be discouraged, I invested in the most popular type of grill in the US, a propane gas grill. Unfortunately, over time the grill built up grease and I had myself a fireball on the deck of my apartment. In a panic, I showered the low-grade grill with water that not only put the fire out, but also gave the neighbor's outdoor furniture below a filthy grease bath.

For years, I overcooked and undercooked every protein put on the steel grates. Even those TV food channels failed to improve my culinary skills. How could that be? They make grilling look so easy! This changed, however, when my wife bought me an off-the-shelf smoker that could only cook for a few hours at a time until the fire smothered itself due to poor airflow. Nonetheless, I learned about indirect cooking from that flimsy flame extinguisher. As a result, I no longer burned my food and everything I cooked from that moment on was deemed edible by friends and family.

Little did I know that other folks had the same issues I had endured. Those of us that are considered barbecue challenged, myself included, find solace on the Internet, where barbecue forums allow enthusiasts the ability to discuss shortcomings and improve our game over the embers. Through this community, I picked up on barbecue concepts and I proudly showed off my smoking skills to friends who awed at the sight of smoke rings and moisture oozing from the meat fibers.

Along the way, my barbecue became refined and I became comfortable with cooking traditional barbecue in addition to the foods I grew up feasting on, which I like to call So-Cal Chicano cuisine. Such gluttonous recipes include tamales, albondigas, mole, and more. This Southern California transplant realized that the Heartland was looking for something like this, so I started my unique style called Mexi-Que. My goal is to blend two traditions into one product and the results have been amazing.

My barbecue competition team, Major League Grilling, formed when my good friend Scott Thomas invited me to compete in his local backyard competition. I've been hooked ever since. The friends I talked to that day are still around and we talk about Q'ing all day long. Competition barbecue allows me to meet new folks and make new friends from all different backgrounds. And while I'm at it, winning trophies is great for my competitive nature.

Not all of us are born into barbecue royalty and handed a wealth of knowledge from generations of ground-digging pit builders (although that would be awesome). I suggest doing the second best thing, finding yourself a friend born into barbecue royalty! All kidding aside, there is no secret to barbecuing; it just takes patience and practice. How do you manage time in your busy life for patience and practice, you say? Start by lighting a fire; drag the kids away from their computers, turn on some tunes, and chill outside with a can of barley and hops. The purpose of this book is to enjoy making the best barbecue in America, so I hope you brought enough cans for the both of us.

Before this journey began, I knew nothing about barbecue. I didn't know the various types of ribs. I didn't know it took longer than one hour to make pulled pork. I didn't know to that pink chicken was a bad thing. Now all I do is talk, eat, sleep and breathe barbecue . . . and I win!

In my first competition in 2010, my team was called Work of Art BBQ team. We placed third in ribs, third in pork steaks, second to last in appetizers and fourth place overall (out of 18 teams) at the inaugural GrillinFools Backyard Barbecue Bash. At the end of that contest, I was exhausted, my back hurt and I was stressed out from turning in the food. For some bizarre reason, I loved every minute of it. But in the back of my mind, I had thoughts that if I didn't do well, this would be the first and last barbecue competition I ever do. Fortunately, I did do well and knowing that I can get better was all the validation I needed to pursue more competitions.

With the help of my wife, Jamie, and my buddy, Tony "MacGyver" St. John, I rebranded our team Major League Grilling (MLG). In addition, for fun I started a barbecue blog under the same name, www.majorleaguegrilling.com. After some encouragement from Scott Thomas, the founder of the www.grillinfools.com blog, I began blogging about my experiences in competition barbecue and Mexi-Que recipes. For the next couple of years, I wrote and folks positively responded to my barbecue musings. As a result, my blog receives over twenty thousand hits a month for something I thought only interested me.

Winning obviously plays a big part of my success. As MLG, we have won awards in all four main categories (chicken, ribs, pork and brisket). Furthermore, I win with the least impressive setup you could find at a barbecue competition. The best description I can offer is that we look like a destitute tailgate party. That may be a bit harsh, but I like it that way. It's fun going up against the guys sleeping in the RV's and hauling ten thousand dollar smokers. That is what motivates me and I have all the confidence in the world in my abilities. As a result, my recipe for success is lots of practice and the desire to work harder than everyone else.

Despite the early success, I have only just begun and I keep improving. There are many proven barbecue cooks that have more accolades and trophies than I do; I tend to look up to them and if possible pick their brains about barbecue. I found that learning from the successful pitmasters is a way for good cooks to become great. Major League Grilling is on the right track, but much more work needs to be done. But I got one thing that very few barbecue icons have . . . a cookbook!

A PIT COOKER'S CREED

There is no such thing as bad barbecue when it's cooked right. This is the only piece of information you should know. Too much emphasis on what kind of sauce or rub you use, or what region of the country you are from, and you'll miss out on what really matters.

Cooking great barbecue has always been—and always will be—about the basics: heat, smoke, and meat.

Let me be clear: *real* barbecue by my definition is smoking meat over wood/charcoal at a low temperature until it is tender and juicy. But I happen to think grilling is also a perfectly acceptable method for adding flavor to various cuts of meat. In fact, for the purpose of this cookbook, all outdoor cooking techniques will hereby be called barbecue. Why? Because I love diverse forms of outdoor cooking and I've spent some of my existence on the West Coast where anything on the grill is called barbecue.

As I mentioned above, the best barbecue is cooked right. Well, how do we know when it's right? Acquiring skills and techniques is the best way to know this. Starting with the basics will help the most inexperienced cook understand how to produce the best barbecue.

Lesson number one: we should all know the internal temperatures for safe consumption.

Internal Temperature Chart (degrees F)
Ground Meat: 160
Poultry: 165
Seafood: 140
Pork (Medium): 140
Pork (Well Done): 160
Beef (Rare): 120
Beef (Medium): 140
Beef (Well Done): 160

Memorize this chart; otherwise keep coming back to it for reference. These temperatures are necessary to know when your barbecue is done. Knowing that, invest in an internal read thermometer. It takes the guesswork out and you do not have to sacrifice a piece of meat by cutting into it to make sure it is done.

I love barbecue because it is a hobby that requires little or no cooking experience. Not every outdoor pitmaster was handed down generations of barbecue knowledge. Heck, Dad probably had a propane grill he found on sale at Wally World, not anything to brag about. For a newbie to barbecue, it can be overwhelming. Despite this, the idea is to expand horizons and waistlines because I want to push the limits of traditional barbecue while paying a great deal of homage to the classics.

Lesson number two: the great thing about cooking in general is that you can only get better with . . . practice! That's right, practice, a word that's like fingernails on a chalkboard. At this point, if you choose to separate yourself from the same repetitive cooking style, practicing can make good barbecue great. All of a sudden, every time you cook, the food becomes consistent. The meat melts in your mouth and is juicy, while your skill and "feel" for cooking is enhanced. Practice is a grill technician's best friend.

When I mention "feel," most seasoned pitmasters know what I'm talking about. It is not about cooking barbecue on a timer; rather, it is what comes naturally. There will be a time when you can pick up a slab of ribs out of the pit and say, "It's done." That's barbecue!

THE GRILL TECHNICIAN (#GRILLTECH)

Grill technicians (GTs) are a special breed. These folks are above-average pitmasters who know their way around a grill. Knowledge possessed by GTs ranges from when to apply sauce to explaining the Minion Method. This level of mastery can lead GTs to believe they have better barbecue than any restaurant in the area . . . and more than likely, they are right. How do you know if you're a grill technician? Here are some telltale signs:

- Ability to tell when barbecue is done by how many cans of beer were consumed.
- You cook barbecue year-round.
- You clear snow from the backdoor to the pits.
- Saturday night is reserved for all-night cooks.
- You have more grills than you have kids.
- Foil is your friend.
- In addition to your beer fridge, you have a meat fridge.
- You store barbecue TV shows on DVR.
- You wake up smelling like smoke.
- You turned your cooler into a food-holding hot box.
- You've explained to a newbie that fall-off-the-bone ribs are overcooked.
- You can fabricate a smoker out of a file cabinet.
- Thanksgiving turkey is brined in plastic garbage bags.
- You accrue decorative pig trinkets.

- You have a fire stoker system that looks like the cockpit of a spaceship.
- You believe that every time someone boils ribs, a kitty dies.

And for the tenacious grill technician who also has a blog and posts photos on social media . . .

- Having more food photos than family pictures (guilty!).

This does not suggest GTs are detached; just the opposite. For instance, the time spent around a grill attracts the whole family. Low and slow barbecue allows much-needed time spent outdoors partaking in activities like a relaxing game of washers or cornhole. In fact, neighbors drift over when they smell the smoke, followed by friends stopping by for a peek of what is cooking. Next thing you know, the whole neighborhood is flocking to your patio for some of the best Q around. Barbecue is not only a passion, it builds communities.

TYPES OF COOKERS

Lesson number three: know your cooker! There are a variety of cookers on the market today, but many folks fail to choose the one that is right for them. Mistakes lead to grills being left outside to rust, then placed on the sidewalk for free. Nobody is at fault; most likely the grill wasn't the right fit for the griller. However, a little research would solve this issue. Here are some of the most popular types of cookers on the market:

Kettle ($80 to $500)—The standard in mass-produced backyard cookers. An inexpensive and durable design that has generated a cult culture spread across generations. A kettle is a great cooker to handle direct and indirect grilling for the novice and GT alike.

Drum Smoker ($0 to $500)—Typically constructed using a fifty-five-gallon drum barrel and customized to the pitmaster's specifications. For example, drum smokers can have between one and three grill grates inside, swivel casters for mobility, multiple temperature gauges, and a custom paint job. The options are endless and you'll get the most bang for your buck.

Bullet ($50 to $500)—Varies in size and grill space. The design saves space on the backyard patio and is able to cook at low and slow temperatures when carefully watched. Bullet smokers furnished with a water pan are recommended but this does not indicate better quality. Look for durable materials, proper airflow, and ample grill space on a good bullet smoker.

Pellet ($500 to $1,500)—Designed in various configurations such as kamado, offset, and vertical cabinets. Pellet cookers use compressed wood pellets (available in many varieties), which are loaded in a hopper and burn at a controlled temperature. This is a set-it-and-forget-it cooker. They are somewhat limited on grill space, but convenience more than makes up for the shortcomings.

Kamado ($800 to $1,300)—You'll be amazed at the amount of fuel you will save! Ceramic cookers provide excellent insulation, which is great for smoking meats, but don't go crazy with all that carcass at one time . . . they offer the least amount of grill space. Despite this, kamado cookers are easy to use and will make you look like a bonafide pitmaster.

Insulated Gravity Fed ($1,000 to $3,000)—For serious barbecue competition cooks or catering businesses. Efficient fuel consumption and plenty of rack space for lots of meat are the strengths of this cooker. This set-it-and-forget-it smoker is worth the investment.

Offset ($100 to $10,000)—The quintessential stick burner used by traditional barbecue junkies. Offsets are used by vendors, nonprofit organizations, and competition goers. Be wary of the low-quality offset cookers; a good one will cost you at least $1,000.

You can't go wrong picking from this list of cookers. Once upon a time, I believed that the cook made the food, not the cooker. However, having been an owner of or at least seen all of them in action, I must confess that having the right barbecue pit gives you the competitive advantage if you want to be the best.

Tech for your Pit

Let's face it, a new generation of pitmasters requires the pleasures of modern conveniences. Temperature controllers, digital pellet feed, and insulated gravity-feed smokers have pushed the limits of making the best barbecue with little or no effort.

Temperature controllers such as a Pitmaster IQ are devices that attach to a cooker to regulate the heat inside the cooking chamber. Modifications are required for moderate quality cookers for controller installation, while on the other hand, high quality cookers have inlets and outlets available on the cooker for easy controller installation.

Final Remarks

A quality grill has three basic features: grill space, air flow controls, and a way to separate ashes from lit coals. Drum smokers are usually constructed out of a fifty-five-gallon steel drum and plans to build them are rampant on the Internet. Designs vary widely and only your imagination can hold you back. So go ahead and mount that bottle opener or attach that oversized chrome exhaust pipe because it's going to look cool. Do not be intimidated by jumbo or fancy grills. Some of the best barbecue I ever had was produced in a handmade fifty-five-gallon-drum barrel smoker.

BEST MEATS TO BARBECUE

Doesn't meat taste better when it is cooked over an open flame? Which is your favorite? I conducted a social media poll and the results found that tri tip, spareribs, and rib-eye steaks were in a virtual tie to be the best meat to barbecue! Are you just as surprised as I am? Well here's more meat that popped up on the radar (not in any particular order):

Pork steaks
Beef tenderloin
Brisket
Skirt steak
Pork shoulder

Chuck roast
Pork tenderloin
Pork belly
Beef ribs
Teres major steaks

Be certain you will find recipes in this book containing these succulent meats and many other cuts as well. The next time you are carefully observing a stocked meat case at the market, try one of these best meats to barbecue. You won't be disappointed.

GOT WOOD?

What is the difference between good barbecue and *great* barbecue? Smoke! When a thin blue mist starts to rise out of the smoker, my taste buds get happy. Do not be fooled unless you see a smoke ring around the meat—that is real barbecue! No amount of rub or sauce can take the place of a piece of meat properly seasoned with smoke. However, just like barbecue rubs and sauces can be applied excessively, so too can smoke. It is important to balance all three elements to achieve great barbecue.

My wood chunk pile has only my favorite types of wood:

Apple
Cherry
Peach
Hickory
Oak
Pecan
Maple

The one attribute they share on my taste palate is that each one produces a mild discharge of smoke. Any one of these types of wood will complement a wide range of food on the grill, from vegetables to seafood to meats. Overpowering woods such as cedar and mesquite are not what I like in my 'cue; however, if you use it, do it sparingly.

To find good wood for barbecue, check your local meat market, a hearth and fireplace store, or a store dedicated to selling barbecue supplies. There are a lot of online retailers that sell quality smoke wood and the prices are reasonable. In addition, I've seen wood for barbecue advertised on Craigslist. If the ad is legit, you may score some inexpensive and locally cut timber for the smoker. Try to avoid the big box hardware stores and retail chain stores. Their wood chunks and chips lack quality and can ruin a perfectly beautiful piece of meat on the grill.

Recently, using wood on all types of grills has reached rock star status—everybody is crazy for smoke rings. As a result, the private sector has responded with more ways to infuse smoke into your barbecue than ever before. For example, compressed wood created a niche with pellet cooker enthusiasts and now compressed woods are sold in chunks and larger sizes to meet demand. Furthermore, an influx of new types of wood chips are being introduced to barbecue, such as sassafras, apricot, grape, alder, pear, citrus, and so many more.

Once in a while, I get asked a question about soaking wood in water. I have never done that, because I don't want to create moisture by sacrificing smoke. There are other ways to get moisture in the cook chamber (i.e. a water pan). Again, that is one of those traditional techniques some folks want to hold on to and is divisive among pitmasters. Overall, smoldering chunks of timber is not optional anymore; it is permanently part of the flavor profile.

IT'S ALL ABOUT THE RIBS

Pork ribs are the flagship of barbecue, a Titian masterpiece on steel grates, the *Citizen Kane* seasoned by smoke and by all accounts . . . delicioso! Every patio warrior has at least attempted to tenderize this unforgiving rack of enjoyment. From my experience working with novice grill technicians, the success rate for succulent ribs is about 50/50.

Therefore, I present to you the most thorough education on preparing the best ribs ever seen in print. This monstrous tutorial about ribs is made possible by the long list of rib recipes on cable TV selling its viewers empty promises of tender, juicy ribs. Similarly, details for cooking pork spare ribs have been underserved and shrouded in smoke in numerous cookbooks dedicated to the swine slabs. Lastly, the best cooking class doesn't always reveal all its secrets and the paying customers are often left to read between the lines.

Are you picking up what I'm putting down? Let's get started!

My Instruments

Here are my weapons of choice when I barbecue ribs from start to finish (minus the ingredients, which will be discussed below). They include what I use to prepare a fire, maintain the grill, prepare the meat, and cook to perfection:

Charcoal grill
Charcoal lump or briquettes
Charcoal chimney
Grill brush
Ash shovel
Silicone baste brush
Long spatula and tongs
Heat resistant gloves
Lighter
Newspaper/charcoal bag
Butcher's knife
Aluminum foil
Paper towels
Large cutting board
Chunks of smoke wood
Barbecue utility table

Depending on what type of cooker you have, the list of items should vary a little. In addition, meat thermometers are optional because I don't tend to take the temperature of the ribs. Instead, I use techniques to feel and see when the ribs are done. More about that will be discussed later.

Rib Selection

When pitmasters start talking ribs, it only implies *pork* ribs. Specifically two cuts of pork ribs: spareribs and loin back ribs. Beef ribs or any other type of protein ribs are considered a regional delicacy. Even though ancillary ribs are tasty, authentic ribs are considered only from hogs.

Spareribs are rather fatty, meaty, and shaped irregularly. They are cut from a section of the hog, the pork belly, which is commonly made into bacon—a good indication of flavorful ribs. From the underside of the ribs, the bones are clearly visible on the slab. However, surrounding the bones is excess meat and cartilage. Most folks just trim this part off to make a clean, rectangular piece of meat. When this is done, the ribs are called St. Louis-Style. Pre-cut St. Louis-style ribs are now commonly found in the meat section of your grocery store, but be prepared to pay more for something that only takes a couple of minutes to do yourself. Moreover, don't think about throwing away the trimmings because you can make them into a delicacy known to the barbecue community as rib tips.

We all know the annoying (yet catchy!) song, "I want my baby back baby back baby back ribs." While the tune sent the crowds craving baby back ribs, the barbecue community gladly stockpiled spareribs for slow-smoking goodness. Baby back ribs come from near the spine of the hog, where the loin (a lean cut of pork) is located. Typically, you may find the larger version called loin back ribs in a package at the grocery store, or you may be fortunate enough to find the baby backs in the meat case at your local meat market. Loin backs are meaty and it is a leaner muscle compared to spareribs. As a result, they lack the flavor but are still a good eat!

I recommend that you try a St. Louis-style rack of ribs and a loin back rack of ribs to see which type of ribs you like best. There are pros and cons for each, but I've gotten excellent feedback using both. This choice is a popular point of debate in the barbecue-community. To me, it doesn't matter because it's all about how they look and taste.

When I'm selecting ribs for competition, I'm going with the rack that looks meatier, has more fat, has straight bones, and resembles close to a perfect rack of ribs. Also, don't be afraid to buy the vacuum-sealed ribs from a warehouse club store. They are excellent quality. Considering my ribs are being judged with prizes and braggin' rights at stake, I absolutely avoid meager ribs. Meager ribs are not worth the six hours of smoke paradise.

Additional Notes about Ribs

Keep in mind that baby back ribs weigh less than two pounds, and anything above that are loin back ribs. In addition, spareribs are trimmed to make St. Louis-style ribs. Thus, St. Louis-Style has nothing to do with how they are cooked.

Furthermore, loin backs ribs or St. Louis-style ribs benefit most from the 3-2-1 method (which you will learn about below).

Trimming/Removing Membrane

Trimming is the initial step of the process in preparing ribs. When you buy pork ribs, they are not usually ready to cook immediately. There are a couple of things to look for to see if trimming is necessary; first, do the ribs have a membrane? The membrane is a thin but tough white translucent film on the bone side of the rack of ribs. Rarely can you find ribs without the membrane.

If a butcher is available, politely ask him to remove the membrane for you. However, I suggest learning this technique yourself because it is an easy process to execute at home. For me, the best way to remove it is by prying up the edge of the membrane with a butter knife, against the last end rib bone. When enough of the membrane is pried off to pinch with your fingers, use a paper towel for gripping and peel off the slimy membrane across the slab. This may take just one attempt, or sometimes a few, before you remove the whole membrane.

Once the membrane is removed, if these are loin back ribs (or baby back ribs), nothing else is left to trim—it is time to smoke 'em! There are several options for spareribs. Whole spareribs are an irregular mass of meat that was cut from the pork belly. In different regions of the country, spareribs are cooked whole. However, most pitmasters prefer to prepare barbecue ribs in the St. Louis-Style. This style removes the cartilage surrounding the bones and shapes the ribs into a uniform size for even cooking.

Seasoning Ribs

The importance of flavoring ribs with sugars, herbs, and spices cannot be emphasized enough. Pork ribs already have great flavor because of the natural fat that is found between the bones and throughout the slab. But when combined with seasonings, the meat is enhanced and the surface develops a crust full of flavor. That exterior crust is commonly known as the bark. The bark is a prized condiment that adds complex flavors and textures. The casual barbecue connoisseur may see a burnt rack of ribs while the barbecue enthusiast sees a perfectly smoked slab. Ribs coated in a brown sugar-based rub and then smoked for hours display a sexy caramelization of sugars that showcases mahogany perfection. This is called the Maillard reaction for all you foodie geeks!

Each grill tech has his or her own technique of seasoning ribs; consequently, some apply a heavy coat while others lightly dust. Even more, the amount of time to wait after applying the rub is a hotly contested subject in itself! You may hear one person say that covering in plastic wrap overnight works best while another says to start cooking directly after the rub application. There is no wrong way to season ribs, just be sure to do it if you want ribs done right!

Since this is my show, so to speak, I am more than happy to weigh in on this divisive subject. I like to season my ribs with a light coat of rub until it looks wet. Apply a second coat of rub and repeat with a third. For approximately one hour, let the ribs set at room temperature, drawing in the spices of the rub. They are now ready for cooking.

Marinades, Injections, and Brines

To a lesser extent, liquid-based flavor enhancers serve as another layer of flavor and means to retain moisture throughout the cooking process. While many grill techs experiment with these techniques, the end product meets with mixed results. For example, brined ribs have a tendency to taste like ham and the marinades do not seem to penetrate the meat enough to infuse more flavor. Not all liquid methods will end up with these results. Some folks swear by this method, and I am a believer.

Best Methods to Cook Ribs

Arguably, barbecued ribs are deeply rooted in the fabric of American cuisine. Therefore, I consider slow smoking to be the ideal method for this cut of meat. However, that does not mean other methods are inferior; on the contrary, they are meant to conveniently transform a tough cut of meat that can be enjoyed. Some methods are better than others, in my experience, but don't let that stop you if you find another technique that works.

Indirect Heat: Ol' fashioned smoking. There is a reason that summer weekend warriors fire up their grill for ribs, to smoke 'em until they are tender. It's impossible to duplicate both the texture and aroma of a well-smoked slab on anything inside the house. The only way to achieve this is applying indirect heat, which typically is offset or buffered by a heat shield or water pan over an open flame.

To those hardcore grill techs that use only charcoal or wood: please avert your eyes from reading further or skip to the next section.

Folks that use propane and natural gas grills can also benefit from the indirect heat method. By using the same approach as on a charcoal grill, cooking with gas can achieve the same tender and flavorful ribs. However, to say that this type of cooking can compete with smoke is like saying Salisbury steak tastes like a ribeye. Please turn in your grill tech card.

Avoid

Parboiling: Purists pronounce, "Sacrilege!" In the realm of cooking ribs, avoid boiling at all cost. Sure, heating ribs in a pot full of water will tenderize the meat, but all the flavor, texture, and appearance will be compromised. To hardcore barbecue snobs (like myself), it is not worth the degradation of such a costly cut of meat. With that said, it's all about personal preference. Boil away if you wish.

Direct Heat: Will not work because ribs have connective tissue that needs time to break down. By the time the ribs are hot enough to tenderize on the inside, the surface of the meat will be charred and tough.

Best Cooking Temperature for Ribs

Connective tissue and cartilage woven into ribs make this an unforgiving cut of meat. Hours of exposure to low heat have long been the traditional way to cook ribs. Low and slow is still the standard, but recently higher temps, but not grilling temps, are becoming chic for achieving sublime tenderness.

Low and Slow Smoking: 225–275 degrees F—Picture the old days on Saturday when Pop fires up the smoker, opens up a case of beer, and measures time with empty cans. You can't look at the clock when barbecuing; it's done when it's done. That's my kind of cooking and it's still widely considered "real" barbecue. We're doing our part towards keeping tradition alive.

Hot and Fast Smoking: 300–350 degrees F—Need ribs in a pinch or done at a certain time?

These temps are low enough to be considered barbecue and results have shown to be championship quality—literally! Try it, you won't be disappointed.

Grilling: 450+ degrees F—Ideal for roasting ribs, not barbecue. Temps this high are not unheard of and a well-known Memphis rib establishment made a name for themselves doing this. I have had excellent results cooking ribs at these temps.

Complementary Wood for Ribs

When ribs are served at the local barbecue joint, focus is commonly on the dry rub and the sauce. What about the smoke? A decent rib shack knows a thing or two about its own product, so when a blank stare comes across the server's face when posing such a question, cordially leave the grounds and never return. Smoke is the essence for authentic ribs; it completes the trifecta of a full flavored rack.

Choose your smoke wisely, or else overpowering ribs is subjected to the barbecue penalty box. More subtle smoke such as fruit wood varieties—apple, cherry, and peach—are excellent for ribs. In the same regard, pecan and maple are pleasant as well. Notice I left out two traditionally dominant smoke woods, hickory and oak. Unless hickory or oak are found locally, pass on the stuff found in the retail chain stores.

Rib Accessories

As popular as ribs are to weekend warriors, few gadgets and gizmos exist for the savory slab of pork.

The most prominent accessory for ribs, and most replicated, is the rib rack. A rack can load multiple bands of ribs while saving valuable cooking space on the grill. While looking like nothing more than napkin holders attached together, the device is inexpensive and does its job for those with little room to lay ribs flat on the grates. Using one isn't difficult either; the slabs are slotted side by side while standing vertically. As a result, the advantage is using the thickness of the ribs and not the width to create room on the grill.

A lesser-known accessory is the rotisserie rib cooking device. This version is not the typical rotisserie where you puncture the meat through a spit. Instead, a rib rotisserie has trays to lay the slabs flat while cooking. Furthermore, ribs are not the only meat you can use on this gadget. Try chicken wings, hamburgers, potatoes, and sausages too! Rotisserie cooking is a great way to produce flavorful ribs because the meat drippings baste the ribs as they rotate around and around.

Overcooking vs. Undercooking

The most common error grill technicians make is not cooking the ribs long enough.

A popular misconception is that tough ribs are overcooked. Not true. Tough ribs are due to undercooking the rack. Unlike other large cuts of meat like roasts, rounds, or tenderloins, ribs do not get tough at a higher internal cooking temp. On the contrary, due to their high concentration of connective tissue, fat, and collagen, ribs become tender with a higher internal temp.

Doneness Tests

There are several ways to check to make sure your smoked ribs are tender. Here are a few ways to tell:

- The first indication is when the meat pulls back about a quarter inch from the bone (some pull back more than others).
- Take a toothpick and poke between the bones at the thickest part of the ribs. If it easily slides in and out of the rack, it's done.
- With a pair of tongs, grab one end of the ribs. If they bend easily they are done; if not, keep them in the cooker.

Not one test will determine whether the ribs are done. Use a combination of all three. I promise that these tried and true techniques can help you achieve tender ribs bliss!

The Perfect Bite

A perfect bite is made up of three components; tenderness, moisture, and flavor. Tenderness for ribs is the delicate balance of not overcooking to the point of becoming mush. On the other hand, undercooking ribs renders the slabs tough and chewy, like a two-dollar steak.

Ribs must be moist; this means that the juices can be seen in the meat. When the fat is properly rendered, it flavors and bastes the meat to juicy perfection. However, nothing is more unpleasant than dry or tough ribs when you bite into them.

Sweet palates rule ribs because sweetness unquestionably complements this cut of meat best. Do not be mistaken that pouring honey all over ribs will make you grand champion—it won't. A combination of sweet, salty, tang, and heat needs to be utilized to achieve a flawless balance of flavors to offset the pure sweet taste.

Once you meet all the criteria above, having ribs with the perfect bite is easily achieved and something to be proud of.

3-2-1 Spareribs Method

What is 3-2-1?

3-2-1 represents the number of hours a rack of spareribs cooks at each stage. In other words, the ribs smoke for three hours, wrap for two hours, and cook without smoke for the last hour. Total, the ribs will spend six hours on the cooker. Do not use this technique on country ribs or beef ribs. It doesn't work as well because the country ribs are too lean and the cook times along with the flavor profile are all wrong for beef. Details of this are broken down even further as you continue to read.

The Plan

Basically, the 3-2-1 method calls for a simple list of ingredients that are applied at different steps in the process. This list of essentials includes:

Ribs

Barbecue rub

Liquids such as apple juice (for foil wrap)

Barbecue sauce

Canola oil

Sure, this list is short, but the ingredients themselves are complex and broad.

Step 1

If the ribs are frozen, thaw them out for approximately 3 to 4 days in the refrigerator. On the day of the cook, let the unfrozen ribs come to room temperature. While the ribs are sitting out, coat them with canola oil, then apply a sweet, sugar-based rub to the ribs by gently patting the rub into the meat. Let it sit until the rub turns into a syrup glaze.

During this time, prepare the cooker for smoking. You should have a smoker or a charcoal grill to cook ribs. If you have a charcoal grill, use the two-zone method. Set the temperature of the grill to approximately 225 degrees Fahrenheit.

Note: I have done ribs on a gas grill and they turned out just fine.

Step 2

Wait about 20 to 30 minutes for the temperature to stabilize at 225 degrees F. Add the glazed rack of ribs to the cooker, flesh side up. Remember, always keep the lid on or closed with the vents wide open.

Add 2 or 3 chunks of dry seasoned hardwood or fruit wood to the smoker. Refer back to page 7 for wood suggestions.

Let the ribs smoke for 3 hours. Check the temperature often without opening the cooking chamber and keep it around 225 degrees F. Also, check the charcoal and water/liquids as necessary.

Note: One element to achieve tender, moist ribs is a source of water in the cooking chamber. Humidity keeps the moisture inside the ribs. Typically, large trailer smokers create moisture by cooking large quantities of meat, but one or two racks of ribs cannot produce moisture in the grill. So, adding a pan of water directly over the heat source or next to it can recreate that moisture.

Step 3

At 3 hours, the ribs could be considered ready to eat. But the connective tissue has not broken down at this point. If you ate the ribs now they would be tough and chewy. This next step will accelerate the breakdown of connective tissue, which will result in a tender product.

When the 3 hours are almost up, create a flat preparation area. Tear a sheet of aluminum foil, enough to completely wrap one rack of ribs. Remove the ribs from the grill and wrap the ribs in aluminum foil. Before you seal it up, add a cup of apple juice. Doing this will expedite the cooking process of breaking down the meat and render off the fat. Seal it up tight so no liquids leak.

Note: Heavy-duty aluminum foil is recommended because the rib bones tend to puncture through cheaper foil, unless you double or triple wrap.

Place the ribs flesh side down on the grill grate and continue to cook at 225 degrees F for 2 hours. Wood chunks are no longer needed, but continue to add water and charcoal.

Step 4

At 2 hours, remove the ribs from the smoker and unwrap the foil. They should look moist and the rub should appear mealy. Another thing to notice is how much the meat has pulled back from the bone. If there is about an inch of bone exposed, you're in good shape. If not, don't sweat it because it is not a litmus test for doneness.

Keep the foil and all the juices inside of it. Shape the foil wrap into a boat with the ribs meat side up so that the ribs are exposed. Place the ribs back on the pit and apply more rub one last time. Cover with the lid and cook for the last hour to firm it up.

If you use barbecue sauce, now is the time to take it out of the refrigerator and let it sit out at room temperature, or warm it up on the grill or stove. The popular application for barbecue sauce is to put it on for the last 10 minutes before you take the ribs off the grill.

Step 5

Sauce the ribs in the final 10 minutes and check for doneness. Using the 3-2-1 method takes the guessing out of knowing when ribs are done. However, 3-2-1 typically does not produce fall-off-the-bone ribs for whole spare ribs. To achieve fall-off-the-bone ribs, cook them longer in the foil wrap. This will further break down the meat. Do this with caution because the meat will turn to mush and you can ruin a good rack of ribs. In other words, ribs are too expensive to make them fall off the bone. You can get the same results from pulled pork and it's cheaper!

If you want to apply this method to St. Louis-style or loin back ribs, adjust by decreasing the cook times. Use a 2-2-1 or 3-1.5-0.5 method to your desired tenderness.

FYI: If you didn't achieve a tender rack of ribs, cook them longer and keep checking for doneness (see page 13). Better results will only come with practice. No matter how perfect or imperfect they turned out to be, smoked ribs always taste good.

Step 6

Once the ribs are done, let them rest for a few minutes to cool off. When cutting the ribs, use a sharp, un-serrated knife. I cut mine into single or double bones so everybody can dig into those tender treats.

Congratulations! You successfully applied the 3-2-1 method. Enjoy those smoky meat sticks.

Competition Ribs Flavor Profile
Competition Rub

Someone once told me approximately 90 percent of all barbecue competitors use commercial rubs, the reason being that there are a lot of quality rubs on the market and cooks have better things to do than play chef. Truth be told, I am a proponent of commercial rubs and there are many that claim to be championship quality.

Once in a while, I make my own rubs, but my homemade rubs are not quite as good as the rubs on the market. For this reason, I find so many great barbecue rubs at the store that it's hard for me to stick with one. Although, the one constant is Plow-boys Yardbird rub; for several reasons, this is my favorite. Many times I have used the Yardbird rub and combine it with another rub with excellent results. But just for the record, I got first place in a competition using Plowboys alone. Listed below are more of my favorites:

Blues Hog
Dizzy Pig Pineapple
Penzey's BBQ 3000
Kosmo's Q Dirty Bird
Smokin' Guns Hot
Code 3 Spices 5-0

Using a combination of rubs is encouraged. Doing this creates layers of flavors, which is critical in competition. Another trick I use is adding dark brown sugar on the ribs so the sugar can create a beautiful mahogany bark.

Notice that each one of these rubs has a high concentration of sugar. In particular, brown sugar is the main ingredient in many pork rubs. This is because brown sugar complements pork extremely well while at the same time, the low temperature of the smoker or grill caramelizes the sugar and gives it an eye-pleasing look and a delectable aroma.

Competition Foil Wrap

My competition ribs need this step in order to put my ribs over the top of everybody else's. I add a special combination of rich ingredients to go into my wrap. With these ingredients, I've taken third, second, and first place, so the judges obviously like the flavor profile.

Wrap ingredients:

1/2 cup Squeeze butter (such as Parkay)
2 cups Turbinado sugar (such as Sugar In The Raw)
1/3 cup Honey
1/3 cup Sweet chile sauce (such as Tiger Sauce)

This wrap recipe has been used by some of the best barbecue competition cooks in the world. I became aware of it because it's so well known on the competition trail. So chances are lots of other folks are using this combination because it is a well-documented recipe. What makes my award-winning ribs recipe different from everybody else's? Practice! (More on using foil wraps on page 14.)

Competition Sauce

I use a 50/50 mix of Blues Hog Original and Blues Hog Tennessee Red. I like to warm up the sauce because it becomes smooth and glossy. Then I apply it when the ribs are in the turn-in box because I don't want my fingerprints showing and I want to cover up any undesirable blemishes.

The key to a great competition sauce is balancing flavors, but lean more toward sweetness. Also make sure the sauce has enough tang and heat to please the judges' taste buds. Finally, do not over-sauce the ribs; use just enough to complement the meat, rubs, and smoke. Sauce is not required in competitions, but sauced ribs tend to score higher. Although I have yet to know of anyone to turn in unsauced ribs. I won't be that guy because what I'm doing seems to be working. So why change it?

RULE THE ROOST

Let's talk turkey, chicken, and all the yardbirds. According to popular belief, chicken is the fourth most consumed protein to grill (following burgers, steaks, and tubers). However, smoking a whole bird may be one of the most satisfying treats you ever cook, period!

Before you break out the beercan contraption, what if I told you there was a better way to cook the entire chicken? By butterflying the entire bird, all the white and dark pieces of meat cook evenly and stay juicy. First, a little preparation of the chicken will yield even better results. When cooking for an extended period of time, a brine solution can protect that delicate breast from drying out.

Make a Brine Solution

A simple brine solution can reduce the chances of lean meats drying out on the smoker. For this reason, brining is always recommended when chicken breast meat is on the menu.

1 gallon ice water
1/2 cup Kosher salt
1/2 cup white sugar

1. Pour 4 cups of the ice water in a large saucepan and bring to a boil.
2. Dissolve the salt and sugar in the boiling water, then turn off heat and let cool.
3. In a 2-gallon storage bag, pour in the brine mixture and the rest of the ice water and mix well.
4. Brine is ready to use.

Take the next step and add a variety of aromatics such as fruits, vegetables, fresh herbs, whole spices, and sweeteners to the brine. Make sure to check out some of my favorite brine mixtures starting on page 338.

At this point, submerge the bird in the storage bag with the brine. A whole chicken will brine overnight approximately 12 hours. A whole turkey would require at least 24 hours. On the other hand, chicken pieces need only a couple of hours in the brine to absorb the salty solution.

Once the poultry is taken out of the solution, lay it down on a clean surface and wipe off the excess water with paper towels. Prepare as normal because the brine has done its magic. There is no question that the brine helps to retain moisture in leaner meats, but a major drawback to using a brine solution is turning the skin into the texture of a shoe sole. I don't experience this problem much with chicken; however, turkey has produced tough skin after a brine bath. Check out my remedy for this on page 162.

Spatchcock Chicken

Grilling the whole chicken is becoming extremely popular lately. Cooking it whole has a big advantage over chicken pieces: it prevents the pieces from drying out.

Rotisserie and beercan chicken (BCC) are a couple of methods used to cook whole chicken. The rotisserie style rotates the yardbird to cook evenly and directly over the fire. Beercan chicken uses fluids to create moisture and protect the chicken from drying out while adding flavor at the same time.

Unfortunately, I don't own a rotisserie device or a BCC stand. So my solution is to spatchcock the chicken. In the spatchcock method, you don't need a special device to cook the chicken. Instead, lay it flat on the grill with the breastplate and cavity used as a buffer between the heat and meat. The chicken skin also protects the top of the chicken and lets the fat melt all over the succulent white flesh.

1. Start by placing the chicken skin-side down on a flat clean surface.
2. Use kitchen/poultry shears to cut out the spine along either side of the backbone and discard it. (You'll be cutting through small bones and such, so it may require some strength).
3. Open up the chicken to view the inside of the breast cavity. Down the center of the chicken is a small bone called the keel bone and cartilage that extends along the breast meat. They are both covered by an opaque white membrane.
4. Take a sharp knife and cut the membrane along the center of the chicken to expose the keel bone and cartilage.
5. Use your fingers to pull out the keel bone. It may be difficult to remove. Another way is to fold the chicken like a book towards the cutting board. Try to remove the cartilage as best you can; however, I sometimes leave it in.
6. Flip the chicken over, and notice how it now lies flat on the board. You are now ready to apply your favorite yardbird recipe.

Note: Cut the tips of the chicken wings off. They just burn, and that part has no meat anyway.

Seasoning

With or without a brine solution, seasoning the yardbird is a critical step to add flavor during the cook. Just as important is to incorporate the flavors on the outside and the inside, which will compound the effect.

Flavoring with a rub is ideal. Find a rub with a savory flavor profile, one that contains more herbs and spices than a rib rub. For a homemade rub, use salt, pepper, onion powder, thyme, chili powder, and the like, but hold the sugars. If you used a brine, I suggest a low-salt rub for the bird, so it doesn't end up tasting too salty.

Apply the rub evenly all over the bird in these three areas: 1) under the skin, 2) over the breast bone cavity, and 3) on the skin. Be sure to apply some oil over the skin before dusting with rub, which will help the rub brown and adhere to the skin. Next step is to cook this bird up. I suggest the cooking temperature be 275 degrees F for 3 to 4 hours with a chunk of apple wood for smoke.

DIVINE SWINE

Life doesn't get much better than a spending a day alongside the smoker with fresh hunks of pork smoking, basting in a mist of thin blue smoke and cooked until the meat easily falls apart. Pork is widely known as the deity of barbecue, the one true protein far and above all others. With a fine selection of cuts like tenderloin, pork belly, ribs and loin . . . the pork butt has them all beat when it comes to slowly breaking the meat down into supple morsels with low heat, seasoned with savory spices and glazed with sweet sauces.

The pork butt, also called a Boston butt, is part of the whole shoulder. While whole pork shoulders are cooked in prestigious barbecue events such as the Memphis In May competition, pork butts remain the weapon of choice for cooks in most competitions or for backyard bravado. In addition, the seldom used cut of the pork shoulder is the picnic, easily identified because the skin is usually left on and it's shaped like a ham. Picnics are great to eat, but be sure to remove the skin and excess fat around the meat, otherwise the meat will end up greasy. However, keep that skin, it makes for great chef treats (see the recipe for chicharones)!

Generally, I like to focus on the pork butt. This irregular mass of meat has a variety of intertwining muscles with white and dark flesh connected by walls of fat that surround the blade bone of the pig. When I look for my pork butts, I select ones that are about 8 lbs (I like big butts and I cannot lie . . .), that will typically feed about 12 folks. I also select butts with the BONE-IN because when that bone slides out of the meat, it's a good indication that the meat has reached optimal tenderness. However, barbecue lore has suggested the meat is sweeter next to the bone or that the bone helps cook the meat by conducting heat. I can't say for certain any of that is true but it's good enough for me.

Preparing the pork butt

The first step I like to take when preparing the butt for smoking is using my boning or paring knife to carve the excess fat and random bone chips around the meat. I want to see as much of the meat as possible so that the rub won't render off with the fat. But before applying the rub, using a liquid injection is a good way to add flavor inside the pork. Having a quality meat injector (one with a metal syringe) is nice to have in your barbecue tool box; use it to pump some sweetness into all the muscles. Liquids such as apple, grape, pineapple, peach juice, etc., complement pork extremely well and is my first choice for an injection. In addition, adding your favorite rub to the juice makes this a fantastic barbecue injection solution. My basic pork butt injection is:

2 cups apple juice
2 tbsp MLG BBQ Rub

There are more injections to be found in the recipes of this cookbook and each injection recipe can be found under the chapter of Rubs & Sauces.

In step two, I inject the solution into the pork butt. I do this by sticking the syringe in the pork butt spaced one inch apart and continue until every inch is injected. Making a high volume of injections is important because the butt is made up of various muscles. As a result, if you want flavor in every bite of pork, inject often. Also, while inserting the needle, I simultaneously push down the plunger to force the solution in the muscle fibers of the pork. Be aware that doing this will be messy and will squirt out from time to time. To solve this problem, place the butt in a large storage bag and cover the area with your hand while injecting, that way at least it won't hit you in the face.

After injection, step three is rub time. There is no special way to apply the rub, use as little or as much as you want. However, liberally applying the rub on the surface of the pork butt will develop a pronounced bark. For those that don't know, the bark is the caramelization of sugars in the BBQ rub during the cooking process. As a result, the butt should look like it is burnt after smoking in the cooker for hours, but in fact, it's the bark. The reason the sugars do not taste burnt is because of the low temperatures used during the cooking process. Instead, the caramelization creates complex rich flavors one would associate with great barbecue.

This three step approach for preparing pork butts varies between pitmasters. Some have more involved techniques while others not so much. I like to inject overnight then apply the BBQ rub. Others like to inject and rub overnight, while many prepare just before putting the pork on the smoker. Again, there is no wrong way . . . it's personal preference.

How I cook it

My favorite method to cook a pork butt is at 275 degrees F on the smoker for 3 hours. And just as I do to tenderize ribs, a foil wrap is used for my pork butts. A combination of unsalted butter (1 stick) and brown sugar (2 cups) are packed on top of the butt and tightly wrapped in heavy duty aluminum foil for two to two and a half hours.

A cooked pork butt is done at an internal temperature of around 200 degrees. A popular technique to test tenderness is to stick a meat probe into the pork, if it slides in and out like a hot knife through butter, it's done. However, if there is resistance, just cook another 30–40 minutes and test again.

Of course, the telltale sign a pork butt is tender is to cleanly pull the shoulder blade bone out from the meat.

Methods to pull pork

If the pork is cool enough to handle, go ahead a start pulling by hand in a foil pan big enough to contain all that smoked goodness. The meat should easily break apart into chunks and shreds of fibrous muscles. On the other hand, when I'm too impatient to wait (that meat comes straight off the cooker and the juices feel like lava, which makes pulling pork difficult), the first tools to reach for are the forks. Use the forks to tear the pork, but after a while the hands start to fatigue and the scalding juices still touch my skin. This is where I like to use some of the useful BBQ gadgets on the market. A pair of Meatrakes (www.meatrake.com) makes pulling and shredding pork easier and I don't burn my sensitive hands.

When pulling pork, I don't try to finely shred it, instead I leave plenty of chunks with the bark intact. Also, pour the liquids from the foil wrap back into the pulled pork—that liquid contains flavor! Finally, dust the pork with more rub (2 tbsp) for a blast of spice. Most of the time, when I prepare pork like this, folks do not ask for the BBQ sauce, it is that good!

My Competition Pork

Every competition cook has to master the one specific muscle in the pork butt to win competitions . . . we call it the money muscle. The money muscle stretches perpendicularly across and is on the opposite side from the bone. This succulent muscle is easily identified with the pattern of vertical fat strands. Some competition cooks partially separate this muscle (but not entirely) to remove excess fat and apply more rub. This is called the money muscle because the judges love it and it wins the money.

The rules in competition barbecue state (subject to change in 2014) that the pork butt cannot be separated during the cooking process. That means the pork butt has to be cooked whole in order to be within the rules. I select one pork butt in competition to be cooked just for the money muscle because that muscle can easily be overcooked if I tried cooking it for pulling. Instead, I cook the money muscle to slice and those tender discs melt in your mouth like cotton candy. Generally, I like to bring the internal temperature of the money muscle to 195 degrees F, this is not a magic number, but it works for me. Also, just like the other smoked proteins in competition, feel goes a long ways too. The meat should feel spongy, bouncy and juicy. On the other hand, anything that feels too firm or crumbly is not what you want to feel on a perfectly cooked pork butt.

My other pork butt smoked for competition is cooked to pull. What does "to pull" mean? It means that all the connective tissue and fat inside the pork shoulder is rendered down to fluffy, moist mounds of pork being easily pulled apart. The shoulder has many muscles with a mix of white and dark meat. An experienced competitive barbecue cook uses those varieties of muscles to their advantage to show off the skills and to present two or three muscles to the judges. The presentation may come in a combination of shredded, sliced or diced, giving judges the impression of a superior and confident pitmaster. I like using a combination of chunks and slices. But my goal is to never turn in dry or tough pork . . . only tender meat goes in that box.

THE TEXAS METEORITE

Brisket has long been that one fickle meat of disappointment. No matter what I did, that lump of beef, fat, and connective tissue provoked me with the promise and hope to be smoked to tender, juicy euphoria one too many times. My conquest would continue until brisket was foreign no more because he who laughs last, laughs with a mouthful of glorious beef candy. Eventually, the barbecue gods smiled upon me . . . because this brisket is freakin' awesome!

Let that be a lesson to you all. As I have said before, practice, practice, PRACTICE! Now cooking a brisket is effortless and I can explain it all here.

Choosing a Brisket

Finding a brisket may be the most difficult task of this whole process. A fifteen-pound choice grade whole packer brisket is as hard to find as Jimmy Hoffa, so it seems. At the grocery store, you want to avoid what is usually carried: a corned beef brisket or a portion of the brisket flat. Neither one of those cuts is equivalent to cooking a whole brisket.

What you are looking for is a whole brisket, with two muscles (flat and point) attached by a thick layer of fat. I find that the membership warehouse clubs, such as Costco and Sam's Club, carry whole briskets in vacuum-sealed packaging that are excellent quality. A brisket is a bulky mass of meat that typically weighs anywhere from eight to twenty pounds. Moreover, choosing the best beef grade (choice or Certified Angus Beef) makes a world of difference when you taste it. Avoid select grade briskets; they are more accessible in the grocery stores that hope consumers won't know the difference.

Trimming a Brisket

Some trimming should be completed ahead of cooking the brisket, but it is not necessary. Briskets have a lot of hard fat surrounding the meat, most of which will not render off during the cooking process. The best way to trim a brisket is to use a flexible boning knife to cut most of the fat off the flat (top of the brisket) and then flip the beef over to sculpt a thin layer of the fat cap on. Removing the unappetizing grey band of meat and fat along edge of the packer would further clean up the brisket for smoking. Afterwards, the brisket is ready for a dusting of rub.

Fat Side Up or Down?

It depends where your heat source is coming from. For example, in an offset smoker, most of the heat is trapped above the grates so the fat cap should be facing up. The idea here is the fat will buffer the heat that would otherwise dry out the surface of the meat if it were not kept moist with a spray bottle or mop.

Conversely, when cooking on a drum smoker, the heat source comes from below the grill grates. As a result, the fat cap should face down so it can help shield the radiant heat.

Do you feel differently about this approach? That's fine; you are not alone. Oddly enough, fat cap discussions are one of those subjective topics that barbecue enthusiasts love to debate. Fact of the matter is there is no right or wrong way to cook a brisket. At the end of the day, using the fat cap to protect from the heat works for me and I'm sticking to it!

The Stall

The dreaded and unforgiving stall is something every tough cut of meat experiences, and brisket is no exception. Stalling is when the internal temperature of the meat stops increasing in the middle of the cook for hours. As one can expect, this makes many pitmasters nervous about drying out the carcass. However, the stall is common and part of the process that leads to a properly cooked brisket that is delicate and moist. There is actually science that indicates the stall happens because of a cooling action that takes place in the brisket.

Nonetheless, the stall consumes hours and the guests are getting hungry. What can be done to speed it up? At some point, a clever pitmaster figured out a way to accelerate the stalling mode by wrapping the brisket in aluminum foil at the stalling point (at the internal temperature of 150 degrees F). Wrapping in foil retains the heat and moisture, simulating a braising effect. On the other hand, many grill techs do not abide by the foil because the integrity of the bark is compromised. In essence, the bark is ruined by the moisture, rendering it soft and mealy. That may be so, but it's 9 p.m. and I am full from eating delicious wrapped brisket while the unwrapped one is still cooking.

Which side of the fence do you fall on? Once again, another subjective topic divides the most hardcore pitmasters. Do not let your hearts be troubled. As long as the brisket is cooked properly how can it be wrong?

When Is it Ready?

After the stall, the brisket should be watched carefully because the internal temps are going to rapidly increase. Briskets are done somewhere in the range of 190 to 215 degrees F internal temperature. However, you are merely guessing when reading just the temperature alone.

I suggest using a meat thermometer to poke the brisket. If the probe glides into the meat like a hot knife through butter, it's done! Remove from the cooker and open up the foil. Let it rest until it is cool enough to handle (30 minutes to an hour). Opening up the foil stops the brisket from cooking further, which can lead to a dry product.

Alternatively, when the brisket is still tough, remove from the cooker and store it in an empty cooler with lots of cloth towels. Doing this will continue to cook the meat and to further break down the connective tissue. Otherwise, continuing to cook on the smoker will cause the internal temperature to keep rising, which may lead to overcooking the brisket. Probe the beef again after 30 minutes to an hour of resting in the cooler with the meat juices inside. When the tenderness is there, remove from the cooler, open the foil, and rest until it is cool enough to slice.

MY FAVORITE BBQ TECHNIQUES

In this section, I am throwing out all my barbecue cooking tricks explained as best as I know how. Every grill tech has his or her own style and these are techniques I use most often when I commandeer the barbecue pits.

Minion Method

This technique is commonly used by GTs when smoking with a kettle grill or drum smoker because the temperatures start low and maintain consistent cooking temperatures for hours. The amount of charcoal and how much heat you start with is an important part of your cooker's fire management process. Too much heat can turn your food into a hockey puck. Use this technique to build a small fire and over time it will sustain the low temperatures you desire.

1. Fill a charcoal chimney halfway with charcoal (or about 45 briquettes).
2. Pour the unlit charcoal out of the chimney and bank it to one side of the grill (opposite the vents, dampers, and smoke stack).

3. Optional items: wood chips, wood chunks, and a foil pan. Add the wood on top of the unlit charcoal and place a foil pan opposite the charcoal (this will catch most of the fat drippings).

4. Fill the chimney with approximately 12 to 15 briquettes and light them.

5. When the briquettes look mostly white, dump them on top the unlit briquettes. This is the hot zone.

Pit Frying

Pit frying is a technique that I contrived while experimenting with my cast iron skillet on the kettle grill. This technique works well for breaded foods such as onion rings and crusted pork tenderloin or foods without breading like potato wedges and pork belly. The food is first fried in a skillet with an inch of canola oil, then the fried delicacy is placed directly on the grates for a seasoning of smoke, char or both.

I often wondered what fried barbecue would taste like, so I tried it and liked it. I don't know why, but it works! Sometimes all an ingredient needs is a quick pan sear for a flavor crust. The flavor crust is the browned exterior cooked at a high temperature resulting in a crunchy texture and complex flavor. Typically, this calls for little or no oil, depending on how well the skillet is seasoned. Therefore, because my grill grate was not giving me enough flavors on the exterior of the meat, that led me to start using my cast-iron skillet for searing, which creates a brown flavor crust.

I primarily use my cast-iron skillet to create a crust for lean meats such as chicken breasts, pork chops, and tenderloins. I found what I was looking for in flavor and texture. No longer do I care about how cool grill marks look on meat. I just want food to taste great! After all, grill marks are overrated . . . now I'm on the flavor crust bandwagon.

Even more, I love to use the skillet as a deep fryer if I'm cooking a breaded dish. Then finish off cooking on the grill for a unique combination. For illustrations of both methods, check out pages 206 and 264.

Two-Zone Cooking

The two-zone concept is an outdoor cooking technique to create a hot and a cool side on the grill. The hot zone is the heat source, using charcoal or propane for fuel. The cold zone is where you put your food. The radiant heat from the hot zone will cook the meat. This is more commonly known as indirect cooking.

Indirect cooking is a foolproof way to prevent burning the food on the grill. The two-zone method can be achieved on either a charcoal or gas grill. For the sake of equality for those fuel users, both will be discussed.

Charcoal

Here are six steps that will be helpful in setting up the two-zone method using charcoal. Best applications of this technique are for kettle grills, offset smokers, or grills with a horizontal cook chamber. To start off this method:

1. Open all the air vents/dampers/smoke stacks entirely to allow maximum airflow into the cooking chamber.
2. Start the charcoal using the Minion method (page 23), and dump the hot coals into the designated hot zone area. Ideally, the hot zone is on the opposite side from the smoke stack.
3. Place the grill grate(s) back on and close the cook chamber (i.e. put the lid on).
4. Ideal temperatures for indirect cooking are between 225 and 350 degrees F.
5. Once the cook chamber reaches the desired temperature, put the food on the cool side of the grill. You want the heat and smoke to pass over the meat and out the vents.
6. Check the cooker every hour or so to replenish liquids, charcoal, or smoke wood.

Pit Fire Tips

1. To achieve lower chamber temperatures, adjust by closing off the bottom and top vents on kettle grills (or whatever is equivalent on your cooker). Adjust in small increments; closing the vents all the way will extinguish the fire because of lack of oxygen. Vice versa, to get higher chamber temperatures, incrementally open the vents to allow greater airflow to stoke the heat source.
2. The lower the cooking chamber temperature, the longer the food will have to cook. This is great for tough cuts like ribs, pork shoulder, and brisket. Higher temperatures for indirect cooking are great for meats that are lean like pork tenderloin and chicken breasts. Recently, pitmasters have had success cooking at higher temperatures (known as "hot and fast") with the tougher cuts of meat. I highly encourage it, but I'm a low and slow type of guy.

Notes:

1. A consistent cooking temperature can be maintained for about two hours in this configuration on a kettle grill. Check the amount of fuel every hour or so, add more briquettes (10 or 12) if the temperatures begin to drop.
2. Grill marks cannot be achieved using this method. However, you can get those great grill marks by searing the meat before cooking. You need 1) cast-iron grates, 2) oil, butter, or a sugar-based rub/liquid, and 3) a very hot grill, 600+ degrees F. After coating your meat, sear it with the lid off. Then, put the meat on the cool side and put the lid back on until the meat reaches desired doneness.
3. Searing your steak or other meats does not lock in the juices; it only creates a flavor crust, which is most delicious.
4. If you like the meat a little more charred, move the food over to the hot side for the final few minutes or so.
5. Crisp up that chicken skin or bacon by moving it over to the hot side for the final minute.

6. Fill the foil pan with water, juice, or beer to create some moisture in the cooking chamber. Humidity keeps meat from drying out.

7. Using the two-zone method isn't hard on a steel grill grate. The lower temps prevent the meat from sticking to the grate, which over time causes corrosion and rust. Use a grill brush before and after cooking to remove any debris or residue.

Gas Grills

Indirect grilling can best be achieved if you have a grill with three or more burners (side burners don't count). Sorry, no two-burner grills because they're just too small. Gas grills are easier to apply the two-zone method because you can control the temps better. Instructions for the gassers are as follows:

1. Turn on one end burner (this is the hot zone) on high.
2. Control the heat by increasing or decreasing the amount of gas.
3. The opposite end is the cool zone. Place food there.
4. Keep the cook chamber closed once the meat is on.
5. Remove meat when it has reached the desired internal temperature.

This configuration should get somewhere between 300 and 350 degrees F. This range is still considered smoking temps, so ribs can be done on a gas grill!

Notes:

1. To create smoke, use wood chips (not soaked in water) stuffed into a foil pouch. Poke many holes in the foil envelope and place it directly over the flame. Have multiple pouches on standby in case you need more smoke.
2. Again, to char or crisp up the meat or chicken skin, grill directly over the hot side the last few minutes before it's done.
3. If you want grill marks, first crank the fire on all the burners to maximum heat. Sear the meat, and then start at step 1.

Bacon Weave

Everything tastes better with bacon, so make a blanket out of pig candy and wrap it around some meat! Here is how to make a bacon weave. You will only need six steps to get the idea:

1. Lay down 7 strips of bacon vertically, side by side.
2. Fold every other bacon strip in half (it does not matter where you begin).
3. Take an eighth strip of bacon and lay it across the middle, horizontally over the vertical strips of bacon and just below the bacon folded in half. Make sure the horizontal bacon is very close to the folded strips of bacon.

4. Unfold the bacon so all vertical strips are in their side by side position.
5. Fold the opposite strips of bacon up over the horizontal strip of bacon.
6. Place another horizontal strip of bacon and repeat the process until complete.

Use a bacon weave on a fatty tenderloin, pork loin, meatloaf, etc. The finished product is amazing. Here are some additional notes to make a more presentable bacon weave:

1. Use plastic wrap on top of your work surface. This makes it easier to "roll" the bacon around the meat.
2. Use thin slices of bacon because I found the thicker slices give you a "loose" weave.
3. Smoke the bacon until it is cooked through completely. At this point, the bacon is still chewy. After smoking it, cook the bacon over high heat to crisp it up.

Foil Wrapping

The process of wrapping large, tough cuts of meat in aluminum foil is widely known as the Texas Crutch. This is another topic that divides hardcore barbecue enthusiasts. Some folks disqualify wrapped meats as authentic barbecue. For those of us backyard pitmasters without a large commercial smoker, it is essential to wrap because it creates moisture inside the wrap that smaller cookers can't duplicate.

Similarly, foil pans can also be used to hold in moisture. Just cover the pan with foil to have the same effect. However, don't pick a pan that is too large for the meat because you want the juices to come up and all the way around.

Generally, when wrapping meat, you are doing three things:

1. Accelerating the cook time by sealing in the heat and moisture.
2. Adding various ingredients to infuse more flavors.
3. Protecting the meat from over-smoking, which can cause a bitter taste.

There are a variety of ingredients to use in wraps. Here are few ideas:

Brown sugar
Beer
Bacon fat
Molasses
Hot sauce
Butter
Fruit juice
Wine and spirits
Cider vinegar
Barbecue sauce
Broth
Soda
Barbecue rub
Fruit preserves
Soy sauce

The possibilities and combinations are endless. As long as layers of flavors are being incorporated in the meat, how can you go wrong?

Charcoal Seasoning

Seasoned hardwoods do an excellent job adding layers of flavor to barbecue. But have you used other organic elements such as whole spices, fresh herbs, and fresh vegetables? Well, prepare to have your mind blown because I really love doing this with steaks, chicken, and pork loin.

This technique works best using the two-zone grilling setup. Add your ingredients to the fire and grill directly or indirectly. This is illustrated on page 24.

Brining

Brine solutions were discussed back in the poultry section (page 17). I didn't mention that brine is widely used for pork and seafood too. For my pork brines, apples are a perfect complement in the solution. Combine that with spices such as barbecue rub, cinnamon sticks, and allspice berries or refined products like molasses and honey. It's a match made in hog heaven.

Use the same ratios for the simple chicken brine solution to add moisture in the other proteins. Also, use the same principles for soak time: at least 24 hours for large cuts such as pork loin and overnight for cuts the size of pork chops. Seafood such as shrimp really benefit from the brine to impart more flavor. I like to use citrus peels, peppercorns, bay leaves, and garlic because all are excellent savory flavors!

CHAPTER 1

Award-Winning Barbecue Recipes

COMPETITION RIBS

Multi-time Award-Winning Recipe

Serves: 6
Total Time: 6 hours

Ribs are the quintessential backyard torchbearer. Once you master these delicious meat sticks, you are designated awesome for life. My award-winning ribs take an onslaught of sweet and tangy flavors to another level. Much more about ribs can be found on page 8.

Ingredients
3 racks St. Louis spareribs
1/2 cup canola oil
4 cups apple juice, spray bottle
2 cups honey

Rubs
1 cup Kosmos Q Dirty Bird
1 cup turbinado sugar
1 cup Plowboys Yardbird

Foil Wrap
1 cup Parkay Squeeze
1/2 cups dark brown sugar
1/2 cup Tiger Sauce

Sauce
4 cups Blues Hog Original, warm

Instructions
Preparation

1. Apply a light coat of canola oil on all the ribs.
2. Apply the rubs and turbinado sugar evenly on each rack.
3. Let ribs sit at room temperature to develop glaze (1 hour).

Smoke

1. Set up smoker at 250 degrees F.
2. Place ribs on grill and add cherry wood to the fire to develop the smoke ring.
3. Spray apple juice after the first hour, then every 20 minutes thereafter.
4. Check ribs at 2 hours; smoke no longer than 3 hours.

Foil Wrap

1. Prepare 3 foil wraps: 2 sheets of foil for each rack of ribs, long enough to wrap completely.
2. In the center of the foil wrap, layer the ingredients. Place the ribs meat down on the ingredients; apply wrap ingredients to bone side too.
3. Wrap tightly with 2 sheets of foil and cook for up to 2 hours, checking ribs after 1 hour.

Unwrap

1. When the ribs are tender, unwrap foil.
2. Turn meat side up.
3. Cook for 1/2 hour in the foil juices.
4. Spray with apple juice every 10 minutes to keep surface moist.

Rest

1. Remove from cooker after 30 minutes.
2. Rest ribs in unwrapped foil; place in cooler until needed.

Slicing

1. On a cutting board, place ribs meat side up.
2. Apply sauce and brush to coat evenly.
3. Slice straight ribs with slicing knife.
4. Pick 6 to 8 ribs, place in a foil pan, and apply more honey.
5. Apply warm barbecue sauce to the ribs.

Finish

1. Arrange in a staggered stack (4 bottom, 4 top) in box.
2. Turn in box.

COMPETITION CHICKEN

Multi-time Award-Winning Recipe

Serves: 6
Total Time: 2.5 hours + marinating

This recipe has been tearing up the competition recently. It has won me first place twice in the first two attempts cooking the recipe. The results are a rich, classic barbecue flavor with an ultra-juicy texture and a hint of heat creeping up at the end.

Ingredients
16 chicken thighs, bone-in and skin-on
1 stick unsalted butter, cut into 16 slices
Blues Hog Original BBQ Sauce
Apple wood

Marinade
1/2 cup soy sauce
1 tsp Kosher salt
1 tsp black pepper
1/2 yellow onion, chopped
1 garlic bulb, roasted
2 cups canola oil
1 cup unsalted butter, melted

Rubs
Code 3 Spices Rescue Rub
Plowboys Yardbird

Instructions

1.   Make marinade: add all ingredients except butter and oil in a food processor. Mix well, then slowly start adding butter and oil. Store in glass jar and refrigerate. Set at room temperature for 1 hour before marinating.

2.   Trim excess skin and meat from chicken.

3.   Combine the marinade and chicken in a 1-gallon storage bag and refrigerate overnight.

4.   Set cooker to 300 degrees F using indirect heat.

5.   Remove chicken from the refrigerator and set at room temperature for 1 hour.

6.   Wipe the excess marinade off with paper towels. Place chicken in a foil pan, SKIN DOWN. Then apply Rescue Rub inside thigh cavity.

7.   Turn SKIN UP and add 1 slice of butter on top of each chicken. Cover with sheet of foil and cook for 20 minutes.

8.   Prepare sauce: warm sauce on the cooker, then pour sauce into a squeeze bottle. Keep warm.

9.   After 20 minutes, check the chicken and use brush to coat butter evenly on the skin.

10.   Lightly apply Yardbird rub on the skin and place thighs directly on the grate, SKIN UP.

11.   Add apple wood chunks to the heat source.

12. Cook for 30 minutes, checking for doneness at about 165 degrees F internal temperature. Cook for 10 minutes if thighs need more time.

13. Put thighs back in a foil pan and apply the barbecue sauce evenly over the chicken.

Then cover with foil and place back on the cooker for 10 minutes more.

14. Box chicken and turn in.

HUDSON VALLEY BACON WRAPPED SHRIMP

2010 Hudson Valley Ribfest, First Place

Tell You What BBQ (Steven Marx)

Competition BBQ Team (Sloatsburg, NY)

www.tellyouwhatbbq.com

Serves: 21–25
Total Time: 30 minutes

Ingredients

6 oz. Lump crabmeat

Salt and pepper to taste

Juice of 1 lemon

1–2 pounds shrimp (large)

1 lb package bacon

Adobo seasoning

Instructions

1.   Mix the lump crab meat with some salt, pepper, and fresh squeezed lemon juice.

2.   Butterfly the shrimp and stuff with the crabmeat mixture. (This can be a little messy, so have some patience.)

3.   Wrap each shrimp with a full piece of bacon and secure with 2 toothpicks.

4.   Sprinkle some of the adobo seasoning onto each piece.

5.   Cook over direct heat but try to keep the heat as low as possible. I like to let the coals burn down for a while before putting these on the grill.

6.   Grill over direct heat for 15–20 minutes until the bacon is done.

7.   Remove and enjoy.

COMPETITION PORK

2012 Soybean Festival First Place Pork

Serves: 6
Total Time: 8 hours

So many muscles in this category and each is extremely tender and tasty. A sweet and rich flavor profile has worked for me. Always make sure you give the judges samples of the money muscle, which is the best part of the pork butt.

Ingredients

2 7-pound pork butts, bone-in
1/2 cup canola oil
Cherry wood, chunks
4 cups apple juice, spray bottle

Rub

Code 3 Spices 5-0 Rub
Turbinado sugar

Foil Wrap

2 tbsp Code 3 Spices 5-0 Rub
1/4 cup Parkay Squeeze
4 cups dark brown sugar
1 cup Blues Hog Smoky Mountain

Sauce

3 cups Blues Hog Smoky Mountain
1 cup Blues Hog Tennessee Red

Instructions
Preparation

1. Place each pork butt in a foil pan, fat cap down.
2. Trim excess fat around the entire butt, leaving an inch of the fat cap on.
3. Coat with canola oil, then apply rub and turbinado sugar.
4. Let sit at room temperature to develop syrup glaze.

Cooking

1. Set up smoker at 250 degrees F.
2. Use cherry wood for smoke.
3. Place pork butts in the foil pans on the grill.
4. After 1 hour, spray with apple juice every 30 minutes.

Foil Wrap

1. Ready the foil wrap: 2 sheets of heavy-duty aluminum foil, enough to wrap completely.
2. Remove pork at 150 degrees F internal temperature, and place on foil with the fat cap down.
3. Add foil wrap ingredients and enclose the foil snugly around the pork butt.
4. Place meat back on the cooker until tender, approximately 200 degrees F internal temperature.
5. Check internal temperature after 1 hour, and every hour thereafter.

Sauce

1. Add all ingredients in a saucepan and cook on medium-low heat.
2. Mix well and let it cool.
3. Store in squeeze bottle.
4. Keeping the sauce warm is best for applying on meat.

Resting

1. Check for tenderness with a meat thermometer. If it glides in like a hot knife through butter, it's done.
2. Remove pork butt in the foil wrap from the cooker. Open the foil wrap and pour some barbecue sauce over it.
3. Store it in a dry cooler, and let it rest in its own juices.

Pull Pork

1. Remove the meat around the bone (the horn) and slice into chunks.
2. Locate the money muscle (opposite the horn) and slice into 1/2-inch discs.
3. Use remaining pork to make pulled pork.
4. Lightly sauce all pork slices, chunks, and pulled pork with a silicone brush.

Finish

1. Arrange the pork neatly in the box and turn in.

Note:

The money muscle is easily seen before it is cooked. It stretches perpendicularly across, opposite the bone and the fat strands in a vertical pattern. Some competition cooks partially separate this muscle (but not entirely) to remove excess fat and apply more rub. This is called the money muscle because the judges love it and it wins the money.

COMPETITION BRISKET

2012 Soybean Festival First Place Beef

Serves: 10
Total Time: 8 hours

My flavor profile for brisket is enhancing the beef flavor with the rubs and sauces, not covering it up. Achieve a nice smoke ring with cherry wood and make sure to retain all the juices—that's the flavor! Be sure to read the introduction about brisket on page 21.

Ingredients

10-pound brisket packer
Canola oil
Cherry wood chunks
2 cups beef broth, spray bottle
Rufus Teague Honey BBQ Sauce

Rubs

Plowboys Bovine Bold
Kosmos Q Cow Cover

Marinade

3 cups water
1/2 cup Better Than Bouillon Beef Base Paste

Instructions

Preparation
1.   Trim brisket.
2.   Coat brisket with canola oil.
3.   Coat the point lightly with rubs, and liberally cover the flat.
4.   Refrigerate overnight in a 2-gallon storage bag.

Cooking

1.   Fire up smoker to 275 degrees F.
2.   Add cherry wood.
3.   Place brisket on smoker.
4.   After the first hour, spray with broth every 30 minutes.

Foil Wrap

1.   When brisket reaches 150 degrees F internal temperature, remove and place on 2 sheets of foil.
2.   Pour marinade in the bottom of the wrap.
3.   Apply more rub over the brisket.
4.   Wrap the foil tightly.
5.   Place meat back on the cooker.
6.   Remove from cooker when it's tender at approximately 2 hours.

Resting

1. Check tenderness with an instant meat thermometer.
2. Remove from cooker and rest for 1 hour.
3. Store in an empty cooler lined with cloth towels.

Burnt Ends (Optional)

1. Separate the point from the flat.
2. Wrap the flat again and place it back in cooler.
3. In a foil pan, add 1 cup of au jus and point. Cover with foil and cook for 1 hour.
4. Use meat thermometer to check doneness, cooking until tender.
5. Cut into chunks and place back on cooker until ready to box.

Slicing

1. To make an au jus, reserve at least 4 cups of pan juices, strain, and keep warm.
2. Slice flat into 1/4-inch slices, against the grain.
3. Rest slices in warm au jus.

Finish

1. Box brisket with slices and burnt ends.
2. Apply a little barbecue sauce with a brush on the backside of the brisket.
3. Dust with finely ground Kosmos Q Cow Cover on the backside.
4. Turn in.

BEST SPARE RIBS

Award Winning Ribs
B&B BBQ Team
Jeff Brinker
www.brinkercatering4u.com

Serves: 12
Total Time: 6 hours

Ingredients
3 St. Louis-style spareribs
1 cup yellow mustard
1 cup Italian dressing
1 cup Plowboys Yardbird BBQ Rub
2 cups Blues Hog Original BBQ Sauce
Pineapple Juice, spray bottle

Foil Wrap
1/4 cup brown sugar
1/4 cup honey
2 tbsp Parkay Squeeze
2 tbsp pineapple juice

Instructions
1.   One hour before cooking, mix mustard and Italian dressing together. Rub dressing mix into ribs.

2.   Lightly coat each side of ribs with Plowboys rub.

3.   Set up smoker for 275 degrees F. Add apple wood for smoke.

4.   Place the meat on the smoker, meat side up.

5.   Close lid and smoke, maintaining 275 degrees F.

6.   Every 1/2 hour, mist with pineapple juice.

7.   After 3 hours, double wrap each slab individually in foil. Place meat side down and add the foil wrap ingredients in with the ribs. Return to the pit.

8.   After 1 more hour, open the foil and turn the ribs over so meat side is up. Lightly sprinkle with rub.

9.   After 30 minutes, begin testing for doneness and start brushing Blues Hog sauce on meat side.

10. Let cool 10 minutes, and enjoy!

SOUTH CAROLINA RIBS YANKEE STYLE

Award Winning Recipe

Tell You What BBQ (Steven Marx)
Competition BBQ Team
www.tellyouwhatbbq.com

Serves: 6
Total Time: 6 hours + marinating

Ingredients

3 racks St. Louis-style spare ribs
1/4 cup prepared yellow mustard
1/2 cup Dizzy Pig Dizzy Dust Rub
1/2 cup Dizzy Pig Swamp Venom Rub
Dark brown sugar
4 cups apple cider, spray bottle
South Carolina Mustard Sauce (see below)

South Carolina Mustard Sauce Ingredients

1/2 cup prepared yellow mustard
1/4 cup apple cider vinegar
5 tbsp dark brown sugar
1/2 tsp paprika
1/2 tsp Worcestershire sauce
1/2 tsp white pepper
1/2 tsp cayenne pepper
1/4 tsp black pepper

Sauce Instructions

1. Combine all ingredients in a medium saucepan on medium heat.
2. Stir until all ingredients are dissolved and mixed well.
3. Serve when sauce has cooled.

Cooking Instructions

1. Remove membrane from ribs and trim large fat deposits.
2. Coat ribs with mustard and apply dry rub mixture. Light coating is key for this step. Wrap ribs in aluminum foil and refrigerate overnight.
3. Unwrap ribs and throw ribs on smoker for 2 hours at 250 degrees F.
4. Remove ribs and coat liberally with brown sugar. Re-rub ribs with dry rub mix. Return to smoker for 2 more hours, spritzing with apple cider every 1/2 hour.
5. At hour 4, begin to baste ribs with South Carolina Mustard Sauce. Baste liberally (until dripping) at 4 hours and 4.5 hours.
6. Remove ribs after 5 to 5.5 hours and wrap in aluminum foil. Allow to rest for 1/2 hour before cutting. Turn ribs upside down to cut. Apply final sauce polish in the turn-in box.
7. Win.

PORK TENDER BBQ PORK STEAKS

2011 Route 66 BBQ Contest First Place

Serves: 2
Total Time: 3.5 hours

Pork steaks are cut from the pork shoulder and are considered a delicacy in St. Louis, which is home to the world pork steak championship. Lots of folks claim to have the best pork steaks, but I consistently win with this recipe.

Ingredients

2 pork steaks (1 to 1.5 inches thick)
1/2 cup Plowboys Yardbird BBQ Rub
1/2 cup turbinado sugar
1/4 cup canola oil
2 cups Blues Hog Original BBQ Sauce

Foil Wrap

1 cup Parkay Squeeze
4 cups light brown sugar
1/2 cup Tiger Sauce

Instructions

1. Set up smoker at 300 degrees F.
2. Apply sugar and rub on pork steaks. Leave at room temperature until the surface develops a glaze.
3. Add cherry wood chunks to the smoker and place pork steaks on grill.
4. Smoke for 1.5 hours.
5. In a sheet of foil, add foil wrap ingredients and 1 pork steak and then wrap tightly. Repeat with the other pork steak.
6. Cook foil wraps for 1.5 hours.
7. Unwrap and cook in the juices for 30 minutes.
8. Remove from cooker, then brush on barbecue sauce and serve.

HERB, GARLIC & WINE PORK TENDERLOIN

Award-Winning Recipe

Serves: 8–10
Total Time: 1.5 hours + marinating

Ingredients
2 pork tenderloins, silver skin trimmed off
Salt and pepper, to taste

Marinade
1 bottle of white wine
1/4 cup olive oil
1 cup yellow onions, chopped
4 garlic cloves, crushed
1/4 cup water
1 tbsp balsamic vinegar
Salt and pepper, to taste

Basting Sauce
1 stick unsalted butter, melted
4 garlic cloves, crushed

Herb Basting Brush
Wooden spoon
Butcher twine
Fresh thyme, rosemary, and sage

Board Dressing
4 tbsp olive oil
Brush herbs, chopped

Instructions
1. In a 2-gallon storage bag, add all the marinade ingredients and the pork tenderloins. Marinate in the refrigerator for 24 hours.

2. Set up the grill for indirect heat at 450 degrees F.

3. Remove the tenderloins from the marinade and wipe dry with paper towels.

4. Season the tenderloins with salt and pepper, then tie together with butcher twine.

5. In a small saucepan, add the basting sauce ingredients.

6. Place tenderloins and the saucepan of basting sauce on the cool side of the grill. Put the lid on the cooker with the vents wide open.

7. Assemble the herb brush. After the first 20 minutes of cooking, use the brush to baste the meat. Baste every 10 to 15 minutes, reserving any leftover sauce.

8. When the internal temperature reaches 130 degrees (about 1 hour), bring the fire up to high heat (600+ degrees F). Do not put the lid on the grill. Add more charcoal if necessary.

9. Cook the tenderloin over high heat until a little char develops (2 or 3 minutes), turn over, and repeat.

10. Remove meat from grill, place onto a platter, and tent with foil. Let the tenderloins rest for 10 minutes.

11. Meanwhile, chop the charred and seasoned ends of the basting brush on a cutting board and add the olive oil to make the board dressing.

12. Remove the butcher twine, place the meat on the board, and slice the pork into 1-inch-thick medallions. Let the slices of pork get coated with the board dressing.

13. Place the pork back on the platter and pour the board dressing and reserved basting sauce over the tenderloin medallions. Serve immediately.

"TWISTED" BACON CHEESEBURGER SLIDERS

2012 Schlafly World Pork Steaks First Place Entrée

Twisted Belly

Fritz Wiesehan

Serves: 8–12

Total Time: 1.5 hours

Ingredients

8–12 pretzel slider buns

16 pieces of arugula

2 pounds ground wagyu beef

1 green bell pepper, nearly minced

1 red bell pepper, nearly minced

1 small white onion, minced

1 large egg

1/4 cup brown sugar

4 tbsp chili powder

2 tbsp granulated garlic

2 tsp cinnamon

2 tsp cayenne

Smoked Bacon Jam Ingredients

2 pounds sliced maple bacon

1 large onion, sliced

2 shallots, sliced

4 cloves garlic, minced

4 tbsp Twisted Belly's BBQ Rub

1/2 cup dark rum

1/2 cup maple syrup

1/3 cup Twisted Belly's Melon Madness BBQ Sauce

1/4 cup white vinegar

1/4 cup cider vinegar

6 tbsp turbinado sugar

2 tbsp of hot sauce

Cheese Spread Ingredients

1 cup of whipped cream cheese

1/4 cup of Port wine cheddar cheese

1/4 cup of crumbled blue cheese

Smoked Bacon Jam Instructions

1. Preheat the smoker to about 275 to 300 degrees F and add 1 to 2 chunks of apple wood.

2. Place all the bacon in the smoker with an aluminum pan below to catch the grease (you will need this later). Cook for about 45 minutes to 1 hour or until crisp.

3. We prefer cast iron when possible, but any saucepan will work. Preheat the cast-iron Dutch oven over low to medium heat and add the grease from the bacon. If there is not enough grease, you can use vegetable oil.

4. Once the grease or oil is preheated, add the onions and allow to soften for about 15 to 20 minutes or until translucent.

5. Add the sliced shallots, minced garlic, and BBQ Rub to the onions and allow to cook for 2 to 3 minutes. (Do not let the garlic burn.)

6. Add the remainder of ingredients and mix all sugars completely. Make sure that all the sugar has dissolved completely.

7. Allow this mixture to cook for about 1 hour and let everything thicken and reduce.

8. Remove from the heat and allow to cool for another hour.

9. Add the cooled mixture to your food processor along with the cooked bacon.

10. Mix all ingredients until the bacon is chopped and mixed evenly throughout. Do not over-mix.

11. With a spatula, remove mixture from the food processor and enjoy. This can be served cold or warm.

Cooking Instructions

1. Prepare Smoked Bacon Jam.

2. Mix all Cheese Spread ingredients together.

3. Preheat the grill to 500 to 600 degrees F or whatever will allow you to get a nice char on both sides.

4. Start by mixing all wet ingredients (ground wagyu, green and red bell peppers, white onion, and egg). Make sure everything is mixed evenly.

5. Add all dry ingredients to the mix (brown sugar, chili powder, granulated garlic, cinnamon, and cayenne). Mix evenly.

6. Form 8 to 12 patties.

7. Place all the patties directly on the grill (leave the lid open), and allow both sides of each patty to get charred.

8. Once the desired char is achieved, remove the burgers from the grill and place in an aluminum pan.

9. Close the lid on the grill and allow the temperature to lower to about 250 to 275 degrees F.

10. Once the grill is down to the appropriate ambient temperature, place the entire aluminum pan back on the grill. This allows the temperature of the burgers to be monitored more easily so that they can reach the perfect internal temperature. It is a good idea to take the temperature at this time.

11. Cook burgers for about another 30 minutes, depending how much they got cooked during the initial searing. Cook burgers to about 145 to 150 degrees F (internal temperature), or to your preference.

12. Once the desired internal temperature of the burgers is reached, remove from the grill (still in the pan), and allow the burgers to rest for 10 minutes or so.

13. Apply the Smoked Bacon Jam to the bottom of each pretzel bun.

14. Apply the Cheese Spread to the top of each bun.

15. Add a burger to each bun, place arugula on top of the patty, and place the top of the bun on top of the arugula.

16. Enjoy your Twisted Bacon Cheeseburger!

RATTLESNAKE TAILS

First Place Appetizer
Patio Daddio BBQ
John Dawson
www.patiodaddiobbq.com

Serves: 12
Total Time: 2 hours

Ingredients

12 whole Anaheim chiles, as straight and round
  as you can find
1 pound ground turkey, 85 percent lean
1 pound hot breakfast sausage (I use Jimmy
  Dean brand)
1 tbsp Tiger Sauce
1 tbsp garlic salt
3 tbsp BBQ Rub
2 tsp lemon pepper
Optional: 1 jalapeño chile, seeded, deveined,
  and minced
12 slices standard (thin-sliced) bacon

Glaze

1/2 cup barbecue sauce
1/4 cup honey
3 tbsp butter, melted

Instructions

1. Wash the Anaheim chiles and cut the
stem ends off so that they are of equal length.

2. Cut a long V-shaped sliver out of one
side of each chile. Start at the cut end, about
inch wide, and end about an inch from the tip.
The intention is to get them to open enough to
seed, devein, and stuff.

3. Remove the seeds and veins from each
chile.

4. Mix all of the remaining ingredients,
except the bacon and half the BBQ Rub, well
in a large mixing bowl.

5. Roll a tapered cylinder of the stuffing
and fit it into each chile, packing it loosely from
the tapered end up. You want it full, but not
overflowing.

6. Wrap each chile with one of the bacon
slices. Starting about 1 inch from the cut end,
tuck the end of the slice between the inside of
the pepper and the stuffing. Stretch it around
the pepper in a spiral pattern moving toward
the other end (not overlapping). Tuck the other
end in the tapered end of the chile, just as you
started. It should leave you with about 1 inch of
chile exposed at each end.

7. Start your fire and prepare for indirect
cooking over medium heat (about 300
degrees F).

8.   Add one small chunk of fruit wood (apple or cherry) to the fire about 10 minutes before adding the chiles. Wood chips soaked for 30 to 60 minutes will work well, too. If you're using a gas grill, make a smoker pouch.

9.   Dust each wrapped chile lightly with the remaining BBQ Rub.

10.   Cook the chiles indirect about 1 hour and 15 minutes, turning once at the halfway point.

11.   Mix the glaze ingredients in a small bowl.

12.   Glaze each chile on one side, turn, glaze the other side, and cook another 15 minutes.

13.   Glaze and turn the chiles again, then cook another 10 minutes.

14.   Remove and serve immediately.

AWARD-WINNING CHICKEN THIGHS

Extraordinary BBQ Blog (Kevin Haberberger)
Slabs A' Smokin Competition BBQ Team
www.extraordinarybbq.com

Serves: 6
Total Time: 2 hours, 35 minutes

Ingredients
12 bone-in, skin-on chicken thighs
Basic Chicken Rub (see below)
Your favorite barbecue sauce
Coca-Cola (optional)
Brown sugar (optional)

Brine Ingredients
1 cup water
1 cup apple juice
1 can Sprite
1/2 cup Kosher or sea salt
1 tbsp pepper

Basic Chicken Rub Ingredients
2 tbsp sea salt
1 1/2 tbsp granulated garlic
1 tbsp granulated onion
1 tsp ground thyme
1 1/2 tsp paprika
1 tsp black pepper
1/2 tsp dry mustard

Instructions
1. Brine chicken in ingredients listed above for at least 30 minutes or up to several hours.

2. Rinse with cool water and place on tray, skin side down. Combine all Basic Chicken Rub ingredients in a small bowl. Dust the underside of chicken with the rub. Let set while you prepare your smoker or grill for indirect cooking.

3. Roll chicken thighs so the skin is wrapped completely around, and as little of the meat is exposed as possible. Use a toothpick to hold in place. Sprinkle more rub all over.

4. Place the thighs on the grill as far away from the heat source as possible. At 225 degrees F, they will smoke for 2 hours.

5. While they are smoking, heat your favorite barbecue sauce in a small saucepan. If it's thick sauce, thin it with Coca-Cola.

6. After 2 hours of smoking, bring your pot of thinned, hot barbecue sauce outside along with a trusty pair of tongs that will not pierce the meat. Dunk the thighs in the pot of sauce and return to the grill. Sprinkle the thighs with some brown sugar if desired.

7. After about 10 to 15 minutes the sauce should be caramelized and the thighs are ready. Let them rest for just a couple of minutes and dig in.

PACIFIC COAST COUNTRY STYLE RIBS

First Place Ribs
Claudia Hermosillo

Serves: 6
Total Time: 2 hours

Ingredients

3 pounds pork country ribs
1 cup Mojo Criollo marinade
1 tbsp garlic powder
1 tbsp coriander
1 tsp black pepper
2 tsp Worcestershire sauce
1/2 tsp ginger
2 tsp teriyaki sauce
1/2 cup pineapple juice

BBQ Sauce

3/4 of a 40 oz. bottle of Sweet Baby Ray's
    BBQ Sauce
2 tbsp apple cider vinegar
1/3 cup pineapple juice
1/8 tsp ground ginger
1 tsp tequila

Instructions

1. Combine all ingredients except for BBQ Sauce ingredients in a plastic bag and marinate overnight.

2. In a saucepan, combine the BBQ Sauce ingredients and bring to a boil. Let cool and store in the refrigerator until ready to use.

3. Set up the cooker for indirect heat, cooking at 250 degrees F.

4. Grill ribs to medium/medium-well done or about 160 degrees F internal temperature.

5. Just before taking them off the grill, lightly slather them with BBQ Sauce on all sides and caramelize for about 1 minute on each side.

6. After taking them off grill (or just before serving), slather them again with more BBQ Sauce on top.

PIG SHOTS

Award-Winning Recipe
Lock, Stock, and 2 Smoking Barrels BBQ Team
Bill Grenko
www.lsatsb.blogspot.ca

Serves: 12–15
Total Time: 2 hours

Ingredients
1 pound Johnsonville Smoked Pork Sausage
1 pound thick-cut bacon
8 oz. cream cheese
1 cup Mexican four-cheese blend
3 oz. diced green chiles
1/2 cup Code 3 Spices 5-0 Rub
1 cup brown sugar

Instructions
1. Cut sausage into 1/2-inch disks.
2. Wrap piece of bacon around each sausage to form a "shot."
3. Fix bacon in place with a toothpick or skewer several shots together.
4. Mix softened cream cheese, cheese blend, and chiles in a bowl.
5. Spoon cheese mixture into each shot.
6. Top the cheese with brown sugar.
7. Lightly sprinkle shot with 5-0 rub.
8. Cook indirect at 300 degrees F until bacon is crisp (approx. 75 to 90 minutes).

Notes:
1. Need toothpicks or wood skewers for this recipe.
2. Smoke is optional.

MAPLE BACON MONKEY BREAD

Perfect 180! Anything Bacon Category
2013 Rock'n Freedom State BBQ Competition
Gettin' Basted BBQ Team
Brad Leighninger

Serves: 6
Total Time: 1 hour

Ingredients

24 frozen yeast dough balls, thawed (homemade
    is fine if you are feeling up to it)
1/2 pound bacon, cooked and diced
1 cup chopped pecans
1 stick of melted butter

Dust for Dough

3/4 cup brown sugar
1/4 cup sugar
1 tsp cinnamon

Sauce

6 tbsp melted butter
6 tbsp brown sugar
1/2 cup maple syrup

Instructions

1. Generously butter a Bundt pan.
2. Mix together sauce ingredients.
3. Add half of sauce to bottom of pan.
4. Top with half of bacon and half of nuts.
5. Roll 12 balls of dough in melted butter, then roll in dust.
6. Add to Bundt pan.
7. Pour the rest of the sauce over the top and add the remaining bacon and pecans.
8. Roll the final 12 balls in butter and dust.
9. Cover and set on the counter to rise until doubled in size, about 2 hours.
10. Uncover and bake in a 350 degree F oven for 25 to 30 minutes. Let set on a cooling rack for 20 minutes before turning out upside down onto a serving platter.

WATERMELON SLIDERS

Award-Winning Recipe
The Man, The Grill, The Magic BBQ Team
Don Parr
www.donsgrilling.blogspot.com

Serves: 12
Total Time: 40 minutes

Ingredients
1 seedless watermelon, rind removed
1/4 cup olive oil
2 tbsp red onion, finely diced
Salt and pepper, to taste
12 slices Provolone cheese
12 slider buns

Instructions
1.   Prepare grill medium hot (two-zone setup).

2.   Slice watermelon into 1-inch-thick slices, trimmed to fit on a bun.

3.   Combine olive oil, onions, salt, and pepper. Brush melon with olive oil mixture.

4.   Place melon slices on the grill for approximately 5 to 6 minutes per side until they firm up.

5.   Top with the cheese.

6.   Place on the slider buns and wait for everyone to be amazed.

STEELHEAD TROUT BLT

2012 Schlafly World Pork Steaks Third Place Entrée

Daniel Simpson

simpsonbbq.com

Ingredients

2-pound steelhead trout filet

1 tbsp Lawry's Seasoned Salt

1 tbsp coarse black pepper

Sandwich Ingredients

6 soft whole wheat ciabatta rolls

1 pound maple bacon, thick cut and cooked

3 heirloom tomatoes, sliced

8 oz. arugula

4 tbsp Miracle Whip

6 Pepper Jack cheese slices

Instructions

1. Rub trout with salt and pepper.

2. Make a few slices in the skin and put the filet on a soaked cedar plank with the skin side up over indirect heat at 350 degrees F.

3. After 20 minutes, peel off the trout skin.

4. Cook another 10 minutes on the grill, then divide the trout into 6 servings and place the fish onto the rolls.

5. Construct each BLT with the remaining sandwich ingredients, place on the grill, and top with a panini brick (aluminum foil wrapped around a red brick) until each side is toasted.

6. Serve immediately.

CHAPTER 2
BOVINE RECIPES

CLASSIC BRISKET

Serves: 8–10
Total Time: 9.5 hours

This will probably be the largest cut of meat you will cook in your life! But if you cook it right, you will be rewarded with tender, juicy beef slices and nuggets. Even if the brisket somehow doesn't turn out the way you want, it makes great chili meat!

Ingredients

14-pound whole brisket, trimmed
2 tbsp Kosher salt
2 tbsp black pepper, chef style
1 tbsp minced garlic, dried
1 tbsp minced onion, dried
4 tbsp canola oil
4 cups beef broth

Burnt Ends

2 tbsp barbecue rub
1/4 cup barbecue sauce

Instructions

1. Prepare the rub; combine the salt, pepper, garlic and onion in a bowl and mix well.

2. Coat the brisket with oil and liberally apply the rub on the brisket.

3. Set up the smoker at 225 degrees F. Add cherry wood chunks for smoke.

4. Place the brisket on the smoker and cook for 5 hours. Replenish charcoal and smoke wood as needed.

5. When the internal temperature of the brisket is around 155 degrees F, wrap with 2 sheets of heavy-duty aluminum foil (enough to cover completely) and add broth. Cook for 2 hours.

6. Check for doneness; when the brisket reaches 200 degrees F internal temperature and the meat probe glides in like a hot knife through butter, it's done. If there is resistance, cook for another hour and check again.

7. Once the brisket is done, remove it from the smoker and uncover the foil wrap (allowing it to rest in its own juices).

8. To make burnt ends, detach the point from the flat by using an 8-inch knife. Remove and discard excess fat around the point and apply barbecue rub and brush on the sauce. Place the point in a foil pan and cover with a sheet of foil. Cook for 1 hour on the smoker. Remove from cooker and cut the point into cubes and serve.

9. Slice the flat against the grain and serve immediately.

RED WINE BEEF TENDERLOIN

Serves: 6–8

Total Time: 45 minutes + marinating

Ingredients

5-pound beef tenderloin, whole

6 cloves garlic, minced

4 shallots, chopped

Bunch of thyme, fresh

Bunch of rosemary, fresh

2 tbsp black peppercorns

1/2 cup white sugar

3 cups Port

3 cups Merlot

2 tbsp grilling rub (page 330)

Instructions

1. Prepare marinade: combine all ingredients (except rub) into a 2-gallon storage bag. Refrigerate for at least 24 hours, up to 36 hours.

2. Wipe off excess marinade from tenderloin with paper towels and let the beef sit out at room temperature for 30 minutes. Strain and reserve 2 cups of the marinade (discard the rest). In a saucepan bring marinade to a boil, then turn down to a simmer and reduce. Reduction is done when it starts to thicken.

3. Set up the grill for two-zone indirect heat cooking at 225 degrees F. Add cherry wood chunks for smoke.

4. Place the tenderloin on the cool side of the grill and smoke for 20 minutes, enough time to infuse with smoke.

5. Sear tenderloin over direct heat until it develops a crust. Remove from the grill and rest for 10 minutes.

6. Slice the tenderloin into 2-inch-thick steaks and season both sides with rub.

7. Sear the steaks over direct heat on the grates or in a cast-iron skillet to develop a flavor crust, 2 minutes on each side.

8. Serve immediately with wine reduction.

SANTA MARIA-STYLE TRI TIP

Serves: 3
Total Time: 1 hour 15 minutes

West Coast barbecue has been underappreciated for some time, but has recently been getting a lot of love from the most stringent barbecue enthusiasts. Credit Santa Maria-style barbecue for this movement—their tri tips are some of the juiciest and most flavorful cuts of meats to cook over a pit. I've been cooking tri tips for years, but they are still unheard of across the Midwest.

Ingredients
1 3-pound tri tip roast
1 tbsp canola oil
1 tbsp granulated garlic
1 tsp Lawry's Seasoned Salt
1 tsp black pepper

Instructions
1.   Apply the oil to the meat and sprinkle on the seasonings. Dust with a single layer each of garlic powder, seasoned salt, and pepper.

2.   Set up the grill for two-zone indirect heat at 350 degrees F. Add red oak wood chunks for smoke.

3.   Place the tri tip on the cool side of the grill and cook indirectly for 40 minutes or until an internal temperature of 130 degrees F (medium rare) is reached.

4.   Move the roast over direct heat and sear for 5 minutes on each side.

5.   Let the tri tip rest for 10 minutes.

6.   Slice the roast against the grain. Serve immediately.

Note:
Substitute oak, pecan, hickory, or fruit wood for red oak wood chunks.

BBQ PRIME RIB

Serves: 4
Total Time: 1.5 hours

Ingredients
4-pound rib roast, boneless
2 tbsp canola oil
Code 3 Spices Backdraft Rub
2 cups dry red wine, spray bottle

Instructions
1.   Let the rib roast sit at room temperature for an hour. Coat with oil and apply rub liberally all over the roast.

2.   Set up the grill for two-zone indirect cooking at 350 degrees F. Add apple wood chunks for smoke.

3.   Place the roast on the cool side of the grill. Cook for 1 hour or until it reaches 130 degrees F internal temperature. Spray roast with wine after 30 minutes and every 10 minutes until it is done.

4.   Move the roast over direct heat and cook all sides until it starts to develop a crust.

5.   Spray with more wine and take off the cooker to rest until it is cool enough to handle.

6.   Slice into 4 steaks and serve immediately.

BARBECUED BEEF RIBS

Nibble Me This (Chris Grove)
BBQ Blogger
www.nibblemethis.com

Serves: 6
Total Time: 3.5 hours

Ingredients
2 racks beef back ribs
2 tbsp oil
Liquid for foil wrap (beer, beef stock, or water)

Beef Rub
2 tsp Kosher salt
2 tsp black pepper
1 tsp garlic powder
1 tsp Mexican chili powder
1 tsp dried oregano

Beef Mop
1/4 cup beef stock
2 tbsp cider vinegar
2 tbsp beer
2 tbsp ketchup
2 tbsp oil
1/2 tbsp Worcestershire sauce
1/2 tbsp hot sauce
1/2 tbsp beef rub

Instructions

1.   Setup cooker for indirect heat at 300 degrees F. Use oak wood for smoke flavor.

2.   Mix the rub ingredients together.

3.   Whisk mop ingredients together.

4.   Apply oil and season the ribs on both sides with the beef rub.

5.   Cook the ribs on both sides over indirect heat for 2 hours. Mop or baste the beef mop onto the ribs every 30 minutes.

6.   Place each rib bone side up on a double sheet of foil with 2 tbsp of liquid (beer, beef stock or even water). Seal tightly and put back on the grill until tender, about 45 to 60 minutes.

7.   Carefully remove from foil and return to the grill until the color darkens, about 30 minutes.

WEST COAST PASTRAMI

Serves: 5
Total Time: 5 hours + refrigeration

When I lived in Southern California, this little boy loved pastrami sandwiches from the local eateries. No, not the Kosher stuff on rye bread from the east coast, the good pastrami from the Golden State! I still crave that pastrami, but I make my own with striking similarities. I'm happy.

Ingredients

3-pound corned beef (point, flat, round, or navel)
2 tbsp canola oil
Pastrami Rub (see below)
6-inch Italian roll
Prepared mustard
Dill pickles
1/3 cup water

Pastrami Rub

4 tbsp coarsely ground black pepper
2 tbsp ground coriander
1 tbsp granulated garlic
1 tsp paprika
1 tsp onion powder
1/2 tsp thyme

Instructions
Meat Preparation

1. In a bowl, mix all rub ingredients together.

2. Place the meat in a foil pan.

3. Trim the fat cap off, as well as any excess amounts of fat on the surface.

4. Apply oil all over, then broadcast the rub on the corned beef.

5. Wrap the beef with plastic wrap and refrigerate overnight.

Cooking

1. Remove the beef from the refrigerator and let it sit at room temperature.

2. Set up the cooker for 275 degrees F. Add pecan wood chunks for smoke.

3. Remove the plastic wrap and place the corned beef on the cooker.

4. After 2 hours, wrap pastrami with foil.

5. Cook for 2 more hours or until the internal temperature is 200 degrees F.

6. Rest for 30 minutes and serve, or place in the refrigerator overnight.

Sandwich Assembly

1. Slice pastrami wafer thin.

2. Steam 1/2 pound of thinly sliced pastrami in a skillet with water on medium heat for a few minutes.

3. Place the pile of pastrami on a 6-inch Italian roll with prepared mustard and dill pickles.

4. Serve immediately.

SMOKY POT ROAST

Serves: 4–6
Total Time: 3.5 hours

Ingredients
3-pound beef chuck roast
2 tbsp canola oil
Beef Rub (page 331)
1 package dry onion soup mix
2 cans cream of mushroom soup
1 cup water
1 1/2 cups Pinot Noir
1/2 medium Vidalia onion, cut into chunks
4 oz .mushrooms, sliced in half
1 green pepper, cut into chunks
2 carrots, cut into chunks
2 celery sticks, cut into chunks

Instructions
1. Set up the cooker for two-zone indirect grilling or smoker at 250 degrees F. Add cherry wood chunks for smoke.

2. Coat the oil all over and apply Beef Rub liberally on the chuck roast.

3. Place the roast on the grill and cook for 1 hour. This will let the beef absorb some smoke and cook the rub into the meat.

4. In a foil pan, combine the onion soup mix, cream of mushroom, water, and wine and mix well. Combine the rest of the ingredients in the foil pan.

5. Remove the roast from the cooker and raise the cooking temperature to 300 degrees F.

6. Place the smoky roast in the foil pan, cover, and seal with a sheet of aluminum foil. Braise for 2 hours on the cooker.

7. Remove the foil pan from the cooker when the internal temperature of the roast reads 180 degrees F or it is tender.

8. Rest for 30 minutes or until the roast is cool enough to handle.

9. Slice the roast, top with the pan gravy, and serve.

5-POUND SMOKED BURGER

Serves: 8
Total Time: 1 hour, 30 minutes

You're welcome, America.

Ingredients

3 pounds ground beef, 80/20
1 pound kielbasa sausage
1 pound bacon
4 slices Monterey Jack cheese
1 large hamburger bun (9-inch diameter)
Lettuce leaves
1 medium tomato, sliced
Red onion, sliced
Pickles
2 Anaheim green chiles, roasted and diced

Instructions

1. Set up cooker for indirect heat at 250 degrees F.

2. Shape the ground beef into a hamburger patty and place on the cool side of the grill. Cook for 60 minutes.

3. Add sausage and bacon to the cool side of the cooker. Cook for 30 minutes.

4. Remove the burger from the cooker once it reaches an internal temperature of 165 degrees F. Remove the sausage and bacon when the bacon is cooked through.

5. While the hamburger is hot, add the slices of cheese and loosely cover with foil.

6. Place the bottom bun on a large plate; add lettuce, tomatoes, and onion. Place the hamburger on top and add pickles, bacon, sausage, green chiles, and top bun.

7. Slice into wedges and serve immediately.

BOLD TRI TIP

Serves: 3–4
Total Time: 1 hour

Ingredients

1 tri tip roast
Plowboys Bovine Bold Rub
Beef Paste (page 341)
Honey Glaze (page 333)

Instructions

1. Spread the Beef Paste on one side of the meat followed by a dusting of the rub. Turn over and repeat.

2. Prepare the grill for a two-zone setup.

3. Place the roast directly on the grate, over the charcoal. Do not cover with the grill lid.

4. Flip the tri tip once the meat begins to char.

5. Move the meat to the cool side of the grill when the surface of the roast develops a flavorful crust.

6. Apply honey glaze to both sides.

7. Cook on indirect heat until internal temperature reaches 125 degrees F.

8. Remove from grill. Let the tri tip rest for 10 minutes at room temperature.

9. Apply more honey glaze and serve.

BARBECUED CHUCK ROAST

Carl Swartz

Serves: 6

Total Time: 1 hour, 45 minutes + marinating

Ingredients

3-pound chuck roast

1 tbsp meat tenderizer

1/3 cup wine vinegar

1/4 cup ketchup

2 tbsp canola oil

2 tbsp soy sauce

1 tbsp Worcestershire sauce

1 tsp prepared mustard

1 tsp Kosher salt

1/4 tsp black pepper

1/4 tsp garlic powder

Instructions

1. Combine all ingredients (except roast) and mix well.

2. Place the roast inside a large sealable storage bag and pour the marinade over the meat.

3. Marinate overnight.

4. Setup the cooker for indirect heat at 400 degrees F.

5. Place the roast on the cool side of the cooker for 1 hours or until it reaches an internal temperature of 130 degrees F.

6. Over direct heat, sear the roast over the fire until it becomes a little charred.

7. Remove the roast from the cooker and let it rest for 5 to 10 minutes.

8. Slice and serve.

CHILI LIME PRIME STEAKS

Serves: 2

Total Time: 45 minutes

Ingredients

2 prime strip steaks

Canola oil

Butter Compound

3 tbsp unsalted butter

1 tbsp roasted garlic

Rub

1 tsp coarse seasoned salt

1 tsp black pepper

1/2 tsp chili flakes (Chili de Arbol)

1/4 tsp lime zest

1/2 tsp minced onion

Instructions

1. Make butter compound: combine ingredients and mix well. Wrap butter in plastic wrap and refrigerate.

2. Combine rub ingredients in a small container and set aside.

3. Setup the grill for two-zone cooking. Start with direct heat grilling.

4. Coat the steaks with oil and dust with rub on both sides.

5. Place steaks on the grates directly over the hot coals. Cook until the surface begins to char. Flip the steaks and repeat.

6. Move the steaks over to the cool side to finish cooking with indirect heat. Steaks are done when they reach an internal temperature of 130 degrees F.

7. Top each steak with butter compound and serve immediately.

MISSION STEAK WRAPS

Serves: 4

Total Time: 1 hour + marinating

Ingredients

4 pounds chuck roast, sliced evenly into steaks

4 cups Pepper Jack cheese, shredded

4 Roma tomatoes, diced

1 cup red onion, diced

4 cups iceberg lettuce, chopped

2 avocados, diced

4 mission-style tortillas

Steak Marinade

4 cups soy sauce

2 cups canola oil

1 cup cilantro, chopped

4 bulbs garlic, chopped

1 tbsp cumin, ground

1/2 cup lemon juice

1 tbsp black pepper

Instructions

1. Combine all the marinade ingredients in a medium bowl and mix well.

2. Place steaks in a two-gallon storage bag, pour marinade over the steaks, and marinate overnight in the refrigerator.

3. Set up the grill for two-zone cooking, starting with direct heat grilling. Grill each steak until it is medium rare or 130 degrees F internal temperature.

4. Slice the steak into 1/4-inch strips.

5. Assemble the wraps; evenly divide wrap ingredients and place them in the center of a warmed tortilla.

6. Roll each wrap into a burrito and serve.

BEEF SLYDERS

Canadian Bakin' (Al Bowman)
Competition BBQ Team

Serves: 15
Total Time: 1 hour 30 minutes

Ingredients

1 package bacon, strips cut in half crosswise
1 tbsp Code 3 Spices 5-0 Rub
3 pounds ground beef
1/2 tsp salt
1/2 tsp black pepper
1/2 tsp garlic powder
15 dollar rolls (also known as a mini bun
    or slider roll)
Butter
Garlic powder
Onion Jam (page 342)
Freakin' Good Mustard Sauce (page 337)

Instructions

1.   Set up the grill for two-zone indirect cooking at 300 degrees F.

2.   Prepare bacon; spread 5-0 rub over bacon. Cook bacon on indirect heat for 20 minutes or until crisp.

3.   Form beef into patties just larger than the buns.

4.   Sprinkle salt, pepper, and garlic powder over burgers. Grill indirect 20 minutes or until cooked to medium at 140 degrees F.

5.   Spread each bun with butter. Sprinkle with garlic powder. Place on cooker over direct heat until outside is toasted but inside is pliable.

6.   Assemble all items. Build burgers in this order to maximize flavor:

Bottom bun
Mustard sauce
Burger
Bacon
Onion Jam
Mustard sauce
Top bun

TERES MAJOR STEAK WITH CHIMICHURRI SAUCE

Serves: 2
Total Time: 45 minutes

These cuts of steak are a delicacy in St. Louis. Imagine beef tenderloin that is a fraction of the size and a fraction of the cost—that's a teres major steak. In different regions, it might be called a petite tender. I call it delicious!

Ingredients
2 teres major steaks
2 tsp garlic pepper
2 tsp Lawry's Seasoned Salt
1 tbsp canola oil
Chimichurri Sauce (see below)

Chimichurri Sauce Ingredients
4 cloves garlic
2 tbsp yellow onions, chopped
1 cup fresh flat leaf parsley
1 cup fresh cilantro
1/4 cup fresh oregano leaves
1/2 cup olive oil
1 tbsp lime juice, freshly squeezed
2 tbsp red wine vinegar
2 tbsp Kosher salt
2 tbsp crushed red pepper flakes

Chimichurri Sauce Instructions
1. In a food processor (or blender), pulse the garlic and onion until finely chopped.
2. Add the parsley, cilantro, and oregano and pulse briefly, until finely chopped (not pureed).
3. Place the mixture in a bowl. Add the olive oil, lime juice, and vinegar, and mix well by hand.
4. Season with salt and red pepper flakes.
5. Store in the refrigerator until ready to serve.

Cooking Instructions
1. Prepare the grill for two-zone direct grilling.
2. Prepare the rub: combine garlic pepper and salt together in a bowl. Coat the steaks with the oil and season the steaks with the rub.
3. Sear the steak to develop a flavor crust, about 5 minutes each side.
4. Place the steak on the cool side for indirect heat at 350 degrees F. Add apple wood chunks for smoke. Cook for 25 minutes or until the steak is done to medium rare at 130 degrees F internal temp.
5. Let steaks rest for 5 minutes and serve immediately with the Chimichurri Sauce.

BRISKET CHILI MAC

Serves: 6–8
Total Time: 1 hour, 30 minutes

Ingredients

1/2 onion, diced
1/2 green pepper, diced
1 tbsp canola oil
1 pound smoked brisket, cubed
1 can tomato sauce
1 can diced tomatoes
2 cups vegetable broth
1 tbsp Worcestershire sauce
1 tbsp chili powder
1 tbsp cumin, ground
2 cups elbow macaroni
1 package cheddar cheese, shredded

Instructions

1. In large saucepan, over medium heat, cook onion and green peppers in canola oil until soft.

2. Stir in brisket, tomato sauce, tomatoes, broth, Worcestershire sauce, chili powder, and cumin.

3. Bring to a boil.

4. Reduce heat to low, cover, and simmer for 15 minutes.

5. Add elbow macaroni and stir well.

6. Cover and simmer for 15 to 20 minutes or until macaroni is tender.

7. Add cheddar cheese and mix well.

8. Serve immediately.

CHUCK STEAK WRAP WITH HORSERADISH SAUCE

Serves: 2
Total Time: 1 hour

Ingredients

1/2 medium bell pepper (multicolored), sliced
1/2 medium white onion, sliced
2 tbsp canola oil
Kosher salt
Black pepper
1 1/2 pounds chuck steak
Garlic powder
Lawry's Seasoned Salt
1 cup provolone cheese, shredded
2 tortilla wraps
Horseradish Sauce (page 336)

Instructions

1   Set up grill for two-zone cooking, starting with direct grilling.

2.   Toss peppers and onions in 1 tbsp oil and season with Kosher salt and pepper. Use a grill basket to cook the vegetables until tender and charred (15 minutes), set aside.

3.   Apply remaining oil and season steak with garlic powder, seasoned salt, and pepper.

4.   Grill steak on high heat until medium rare or 130 degrees F internal temperature.

5.   Slice steak and add cheese (let it melt on steak).

6.   Warm up tortillas. Add steak and cheese, peppers, and onions and top with Horseradish Sauce.

7.   Serve immediately.

ZESTY-HERB MARINATED SKIRT STEAK SANDWICH

Serves: 4
Total Time: 30 minutes + marinating

Ingredients

2 pounds skirt steak
2 oz. Asiago cheese, grated
4 oz. red onion, sliced
4 oz. arugula
Jalapeño-Tomatillo Aioli (page 341)
4 Kaiser rolls

Marinade

1/2 pint buttermilk
1/2 cup soy sauce
4 cloves garlic, minced
1/2 tbsp oregano, dried
1/2 tbsp basil, dried
1 tsp Lawry's Seasoned Salt
1/2 red bell pepper, roasted (seeds and stem removed)
1 Anaheim chile pepper, roasted (seeds and stem removed)
1/2 cup canola oil

Instructions

1. Combine all marinade ingredients in a food processor and blend until smooth. Pour the marinade into a 1-gallon storage bag and add the skirt steak. Marinate in the refrigerator for at least 24 hours, up to 36 hours.

2. Set up the grill for two-zone indirect heat cooking.

3. Remove skirt steak from marinade and wipe off excess with paper towels.

4. Cook the skirt steak on the grates directly over the fire for 10 minutes or until they reach medium at 140 degrees F internal temperature.

5. Remove steaks from the grill and start assembling sandwiches. Stack the cheese, onion, and arugula on top of the steak and place on the aioli-slathered rolls.

6. Serve immediately.

SMOKY PECAN TERES MAJOR STEAKS

Serves: 4

Total Time: 45 minutes + marinating

Ingredients

4 teres major steaks

1/4 cup canola oil

Salt and pepper, to taste

Marinade

1 cup olive oil

1/2 cup water

1 oz. fresh thyme, rosemary, and oregano

1 tsp beef base paste

1 tbsp Worcestershire sauce

Instructions

1. Combine all marinade ingredients and steaks in a 1-gallon storage bag. Seal the bag and marinate in the refrigerator overnight.

2. Wipe off excess marinade from steaks with paper towels. Strain and reserve the rest of the marinade.

3. In a saucepan, bring reserved marinade to a boil and simmer on medium-low for 20 minutes or until it starts to thicken. Reserve to use as a basting sauce.

4. Set up grill for the two-zone method. Start with direct heat grilling. Use pecan wood chips or chunks for smoke.

5. Apply oil on the steaks and season with salt and pepper.

6. Sear steaks on the grill until they develop a crust, then move to the cool side of the grill and cook indirect until the internal temperature reaches 135 degrees F. Start basting steaks with reserved sauce often when the crust starts to form.

7. Remove from grill and rest the steaks for a few minutes. Slice into 1/2-inch discs and brush sauce over the slices.

8. Serve immediately.

KOBE BURGERS

Serves: 2
Total Time: 25 minutes

Ingredients

1 pound Kobe ground beef

2 slices Swiss cheese

2 oz. artisan lettuce

1 tbsp grilling rub

3 tsp bistro sauce

2 oz. crispy Vidalia onions

2 pretzel buns

Instructions

1.   Set up the grill for two-zone indirect cooking at 350 degrees F.

2.   Make 2 burger patties and season with the grilling rub. Leave a thumbprint in the center of the burger so it does not bulge in the middle.

3.   Place burgers on the cool side of the grill and cook for 15 minutes or until the beef reaches medium at 140 degrees F.

4.   Move the burgers over to the hot side and cook over direct heat for a few minutes until they develop a crust on both sides. Place cheese on top to melt over the burger.

5.   Remove from the grill and assemble the burgers; spread bistro sauce on top and bottom buns, then add the lettuce, burger topped with cheese, and onions.

6.   Serve immediately.

CHAPTER 3
HAWG RECIPES

APPLE CIDER PULLED PORK

Serves: 6
Total Time: 7 hours + refrigeration time

Apples and pork are a classic combination written in barbecue lore. This pulled pork hits the right spot between a classic pulled pork and my competition pork. It's so good, you won't need to smother it in barbecue sauce.

Ingredients
5-pound pork butt, bone-in
BBQ Rub (recipe below)
Apple Cider Injection (recipe below)

BBQ Rub Ingredients
1/2 cup turbinado sugar
3 tbsp Kosher salt
1 tbsp garlic powder
1 tbsp onion powder
1 tbsp chili powder
1 tbsp Hungarian paprika
1 tbsp black pepper
1/2 tsp cayenne pepper

Apple Cider Injection
2 cups apple cider
2 tbsp BBQ Rub

Injection Instructions
1. Boil the ingredients in a saucepan until the rub dissolves. Let it cool.
2. Place the pork butt in a foil pan.
3. Fill an injection needle and start injecting the liquid into the meat. (see page 19)
4. Place the pork in the refrigerator overnight or for up to 36 hours.

Cooking Instructions
1. Combine all BBQ Rub ingredients and mix well. Apply rub on the pork butt.
2. Let the pork butt sit at room temperature for at least 30 minutes or until the rub looks wet, like a glaze.
3. Setup the smoker for 225 degrees F. Add apple wood chunks for smoke.
4. Place the foil pan, with the pork inside, on the grill.
5. Cook for the first 5 hours uncovered. This is when the smoke will infuse the meat.
6. Cover and seal the foil pan with a sheet of aluminum foil until internal temperature reaches 200 degrees F, about 2 hours. Add some liquids if the bottom of the pan is dry.
7. Remove the foil pan from the grill and open up the foil cover just enough to let the heat escape.
8. Rest the pork in the juices for about an hour or until it cools enough to handle.
9. Pull pork in the juices and serve. (see page 20)

SMOKED CUBAN PORK

Serves: 6
Total Time: 7 hours + refrigeration time

Do you think barbecue has to taste sweet all time? No! It can be flavorful without the brown sugar and other sweeteners with which barbecue is synonymous. Latin flavors are often on the other side of sweet—they're savory! Bold flavor is my thing and even better are the Cubano sandwiches you can make out of this recipe.

Ingredients

5-pound pork butt, bone-in
2 cups Goya Mojo Criollo Marinade

Rub Ingredients

1 tbsp Coarse black pepper
1 tbsp Sea salt
1 tbsp Ground oregano
1 tbsp Minced dried onion
1 tbsp Minced dried garlic

Injection Preparation

1.   Filter out the large particles of herbs and spices in the pre-made marinade. I use my fine mesh strainer with a spoon to do this. When I pour the marinade through the metal mesh strainer, I stir it around with the spoon and into a bowl, which results in a homogeneous consistency.

2.   Before injection, place the pork butt in a foil pan.

3.   Take a syringe, fill it up with mojo, and start injecting into the meat. (see page 19)

4.   When done injecting, cover the pan with foil and place it in the fridge.

5.   Refrigerate at least overnight, but preferably over 24 hours.

Instructions

1.   Prepare the smoker for 225 degrees F.

2.   Take pork butt out of the fridge and uncover.

3.   Mix all rub ingredients together and spread it evenly all over the shoulder. Make sure to get those folds and creases in between.

4.   Place the foil pan, with the pork butt inside, on the smoker.

5.   Smoke for the first 5 hours uncovered.

6.   Cover and seal the pork with aluminum foil and continue to cook for 2 hours. Add some liquid if the bottom of the pan is dry. Cook until the meat reaches 200 degrees F internal temperature.

7.   Remove the foil pan from the grill and open up the foil cover just enough to let the heat escape.

8.   Rest the pork in the juices for about an hour or until it cools enough to handle.

9.   Pull pork and serve. (see page 20)

10. Assemble Cuban sandwich (optional):

Hoagie roll

Cuban pork

Sliced ham

Grilled hot dogs

Mustard sauce: blend 1 tbsp regular mustard,
  1 tbsp mayo, 1/2 tsp chopped cilantro, and a
  squeeze of lime

Pickles

Swiss cheese

Butter

RIB TIPS WITH HONEY-GRAPEFRUIT GLAZE

Serves: 4
Total Time: 3 hours

Rib tips come from the leftover scraps that are trimmed off St. Louis-style ribs. These are the perfect snacking treats for the cook!

Ingredients

2 pounds pork rib tips
1/2 cup BBQ Rub (page 330)
1/4 cup margarine, melted
1/2 cup grapefruit juice, freshly squeezed

Glaze

2 tbsp unsalted butter
1 tsp garlic, minced
1/4 cup yellow onion, finely chopped
1/4 cup grapefruit juice, freshly squeezed
1/2 tsp grapefruit zest
1 cup honey
1 cup ketchup
3 tbsp Worcestershire sauce
2 tbsp molasses
1/2 tsp Hungarian paprika
1/4 tsp chipotle, ground
Kosher salt and pepper

Instructions

1. Setup the cooker for smoking at 250 degrees F.

2. Apply rub on the rib tips and place them on the grate. Smoke for 1 hour.

3. Make glaze: In a saucepan over medium heat, melt butter, then add garlic and onions. Cook until soft, combine and add remaining glaze ingredients, and reduce heat to simmer. After simmering for 10 minutes, cool to room temperature.

4. In a foil pan, add grapefruit juice and place all rib tips in the pan. Cover rib tips with melted margarine. Cover tightly with aluminum foil and cook for 1 hour.

5. Cook until the pieces of pork are tender, then cut the rib tips into 1-inch cubes.

6. Brush the glaze on the meat and serve immediately.

Notes

1. Rib tips are the trimmings from pork spareribs made into St. Louis-style ribs, and are filled with bones, cartilage, and ample rib meat.

2. Use any fruit wood, hickory, or oak for smoke flavor.

SMOKED SPRING HAM

Serves: 14–16
Total Time: 3 hours

Ingredients
8-pound butt portion

Basting Sauce
1 cup apple juice
1 cup apple cider vinegar
1 cup honey
2 tbsp soy sauce
1/2 tsp apple pie spice
1/2 tsp white pepper
1/4 tsp jalapeño powder
1 cinnamon stick

Sauce Instructions
1.   Preheat stove at medium-low heat.
2.   Mix all ingredients in saucepan and place on stove.
3.   Remove from heat once all the ingredients are dissolved.

Cooking Instructions
1.   Set up the cooker for 225 degrees. Add cherry wood chunks for smoke.
2.   When the grill reaches the desired temperature, place the ham on the grate flat side down. Also, place the pan of sauce on the grill to absorb some smoke while reducing it at the same time.
3.   Baste the ham every 30 minutes until it's done at 145 degrees internal temperature.
4.   Rest for 15 minutes and slice.

NAKED FATTY

Serves: 8

Total Time: 1 hour 15 minutes

If you were to Google this recipe, you would not be viewing anything about barbecue. A fatty in the barbecue community is a closely kept treat, yet it is so simple to cook. Stuffed fatties are known to exist and the creativity and combinations are endless. No doubt, fatties have a cult following that has the potential to become mainstream.

Ingredients

1 pound Jimmy Dean Regular Pork Sausage
    BBQ Rub (page 330)

Instructions

1.   Remove the casing from the sausage while keeping the shape intact.

2.   Apply BBQ rub all over the sausage.

3.   Place sausage on grill and cook using indirect heat. Add wood to the coals. Close the lid, leaving the vents wide open.

4.   When the internal temperature of the fatty hits 165 degrees (about an hour), it's done.

5.   Slice into 1/4-inch-thick rounds and serve immediately.

MAPLE DIJON PORK STEAKS

Serves: 2
Total Time: 2 hours

Ingredients
2 pork steaks
2 tbsp canola oil
1/2 cup Chardonnay (white wine)

All Purpose Grilling Rub
1 tbsp Kosher salt
1/2 tbsp pepper
1 tsp garlic salt
1/2 tsp crushed red pepper flakes

Glaze
1 tbsp whole-grain Dijon mustard
1/2 cup maple syrup

Caramelized Apples
1 green apple
2 tbsp butter
4 tbsp brown sugar

Instructions

1. Set up the cooker for indirect heat cooking at 375 degrees F. Add pecan wood chunks for smoke.

2. Combine all All Purpose Grilling Rub ingredients in a bowl and mix well.

3. Coat the pork steaks with oil and apply the grilling rub all over.

4. Place the pork steaks on the cool side of the grill and smoke for 45 minutes.

5. Meanwhile, prepare the foil wraps for each pork steak. Use a sheet of foil large enough to completely wrap the pork steak. Pour half of the wine in one foil wrap and the rest in the other.

6. Place a pork steak in each foil wrap, wrap tightly, and cook for 1 hour.

7. Prepare the glaze: in a saucepan, combine the mustard and maple syrup on medium heat. Remove the glaze when it starts to boil. Stir and set aside.

8. Prepare the caramelized apples: core out the apple and cut it into wedges. In a saucepan, melt the butter on medium heat, then add the brown sugar and stir. Cook the apples in the sauce until one side develops a crust; flip and repeat. Repeat for all the apple wedges. Set aside when they are done.

9. Unwrap the foil and cook the pork steaks on the cool side of the grill for 10 minutes.

10. Remove pork steaks from the grill and onto a serving plate. Drizzle the glaze on top of the pork steaks and serve with the caramelized apples.

APPLEWOOD SMOKED BACON

Serves: 40

Total time: 5 days

Ingredients

10-pound pork belly, slab

1/3 pound pickling salt

4 tsp BBQ Rub (page 330)

1 tsp pink salt (Prague Powder #1, a curing salt)

1/3 pound brown sugar

Instructions

1. In a large mixing bowl, combine pickling salt, rub, pink salt, and brown sugar and mix well.

2. In a large non-reactive container, liberally rub both sides of the pork with the mixture.

3. Refrigerate for 4 days in the container.

4. Remove pork and rinse well with cold water. Dry with paper towels.

5. Setup cooker for smoking or indirect heat at 180 degrees F. Use apple wood for smoke.

6. Cook bacon until the internal temperature has reached 140 degrees F, approximately 4 hours.

7. Cool overnight in the refrigerator.

8. Slice into strips of bacon using a deli slicer. Freeze any excess bacon.

NAPA VALLEY RIBS

Serves: 3
Total Time: 6 hours

Ingredients
1 rack of spareribs
Basic Rib Rub (page 332)
Apple wood
Kansas City-style barbecue sauce

Foil Wrap
1/4 cup turbinado sugar
1/4 cup hot pepper jelly
1/4 cup squeezable butter
1/4 cup Napa red wine

Instructions
1.   Set up grill for indirect cooking at 250 degrees F.

2.   Remove membrane from the ribs and apply rub on the ribs.

3.   Use apple wood for smoke and place the ribs on grill.

4.   Cook for 3 hours at 250 degrees F.

5.   Then wrap ribs tightly in heavy-duty foil and add the foil wrap ingredients.

6.   Cook for another 2 hours in the foil.

7.   Next, remove the foil, but reserve the juices.

8.   Cook for another hour or until tender.

9.   Combine a 50/50 mixture of warm Kansas City-style barbecue sauce and the reserved foil juice together and apply on ribs when they are done.

SHOW-ME PORK STEAKS

Phatso's BBQ
Jeff Fitter
Catering Company and BBQ Competition Team
www.phatsosbbq.com

Serves: 4–6
Total Time: 6 hours

Ingredients
4–6 pork steaks, 1 inch thick (18–20 oz.)
Jeff's St. Louis-style Rub (see below)
Cherry wood
Pecan wood
Barbecue sauce

Jeff's St. Louis-style Rub Ingredients
1 cup brown sugar
1 cup white sugar
1/3 cup celery salt
1/3 cup black pepper
1/3 cup garlic powder
1/3 cup dry mustard
1/3 cup onion powder
1 tbsp cayenne pepper

Instructions
1. Mix all the ingredients for Jeff's St. Louis-Style Rub together in a bowl and then set aside.

2. Rub each side of the pork steaks until all pork steaks are rubbed. Then leave on tray or wrapped and store in refrigerator or cooler for not more than 12 hours but at least 3 hours to let that flavor settle in.

3. Bring smoker up to 250 degrees F and have your smoking wood ready.

4. Place the pork steaks on the smoker, add your smoking wood, and close the lid (or door). Remember, if you're looking, they ain't cooking!

5. Cook time may vary (depending on smoker used). At about 5 1/2 hours of cooking or 190 degrees F internal temperature, take the pork steaks out of the smoker and apply your favorite sauce to both sides. Place them back in the smoker and let them finish for 30 minutes. A good indication that the pork steaks are done is to cut through it with a fork, if the pork steak is tough, just cook longer.

Notes:
1. If a smoker is not available, use the two-zone indirect heat method. Use wood chunks for this setup.

2. Find a BBQ Sauce recipe on page 332.

PULLED PORK NACHOS

Serves: 2
Total Time: 15 minutes

Ingredients

Corn tortilla chips
1 pound pulled pork, cooked
8 oz. nacho cheese, heated
1 tsp BBQ Rub (page 330)
2 tbsp crema (or sour cream)
2 tbsp BBQ Sauce (page 332)
1 tbsp chopped green onion

Instructions

1. Spread a layer of chips on a plate.
2. Add the pork over the chips.
3. Coat the chips and pork with cheese, and sprinkle rub over it.
4. Cover nachos with crema and BBQ Sauce, then top with green onions.
5. Serve immediately.

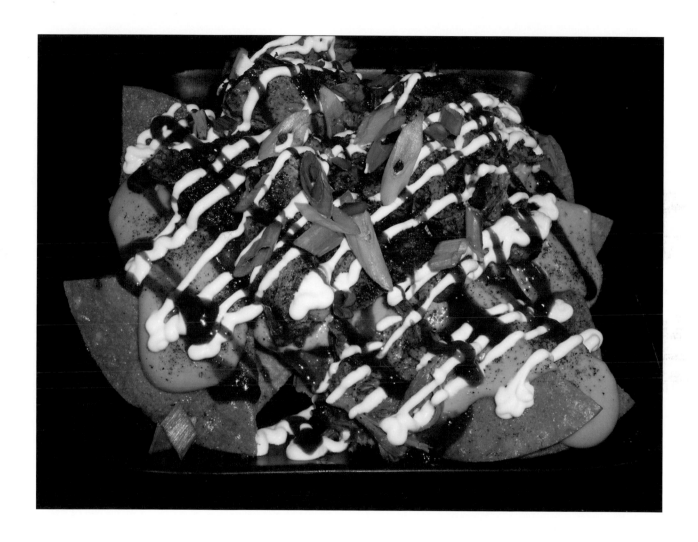

SMOKED PORK SLIDERS

Serves: 8
Total Time: 2 hours

Ingredients

16 oz. package Jimmy Dean regular pork ground
    sausage (in a tube)
BBQ Rub (page 330)
8 sweet mini buns
2 tbsp butter
MLG Coleslaw (see below)
BBQ Sauce (page 332)
Pickled Red Onions (see below)

MLG Coleslaw Ingredients

1/4 cup apple cider vinegar
1/3 cup mayonnaise
2 cloves garlic, minced
1/8 cup white sugar
1/2 head cabbage, shredded
2 cooked bacon strips, chopped
Salt and pepper

Pickled Red Onions Ingredients

1/2 cup apple cider vinegar
1/2 cup water
1/2 cup sugar
1/2 tsp Kosher salt
1/2 red onion, sliced into thin rings
2 cloves garlic, crushed

MLG Coleslaw Instructions

1. In bowl, whisk together apple cider vinegar, mayonnaise, garlic, and sugar.

2. Pour dressing over cabbage, add bacon, and mix well.

3. Store in the fridge until ready to use.

Pickled Red Onions Instructions

1. In a saucepan, bring apple cider vinegar, water, sugar, and salt to a boil, stirring occasionally. Take off the heat and let it cool.

2. In a container with a lid, place onion and garlic.

3. Pour the cooled liquid into the container and refrigerate until ready to use.

Cooking Instructions

1. Setup the grill for the two-zone indirect cooking method at 350 degrees F. Use peach wood chunks for smoke.

2. To prepare the pork sausage, follow instructions for the Naked Fatty on page 116.

3. Toast the rolls by spreading butter on the top and bottom buns and then grilling them directly over the heat with a hint of char.

4. Slice the fatty into round discs, about one inch thick, to be placed flat on the bun.

5. To assemble the sliders: place a pork disc on the grilled bottom bun, then place a spoonful of coleslaw on top of the fatty disc. Drizzle a good dose of BBQ sauce over the slaw and finish off with a few dripping rings of pickled onions.

6. Serve immediately.

CRISPY PORK TENDERLOIN SANDWICH

Serves: 4
Total Time: 1 hour

Crispy Pork Ingredients

1 pork tenderloin (approximately 1 pound)
Vegetable oil
1/2 cup flour
2 eggs (beaten to make an egg wash)
2 cups panko

Instructions

1. Cut the tenderloin into 4 equally sized sections.
2. Pound the tenderloin sections to a 1/4-inch thickness and into a round shape.
3. Set up the cooker for two-zone direct grilling. Place a large cast-iron skillet directly over the heat, approximately at 450 degrees F.
4. Add vegetable oil to 1/8-inch depth
5. Coat the flattened pork in flour.
6. Dredge the pork through the egg wash.
7. Coat the pork in panko and place in the hot skillet.
8. Cook until golden brown for 3 minutes on each side.
9. Remove pork from skillet and place on paper towel.

Sandwich Ingredients

1 crusty baguette bread
4 tbsp mayonnaise
2 tsp Frank's Red Hot sauce
Crispy Pork
Dill pickles
White onion, sliced

Instructions

1. Cut the baguette into 4 sections to use as buns.
2. Combine mayo with a few shots of hot sauce and spread on the baguette.
3. Stack the rest of the ingredients between the bread slices and serve.

BLOW-TORCHED RIBS

Grillin' Fools
Scott Thomas
BBQ Blogger
www.grillinfools.com

Serves: 6
Total time: 2 hours, 30 minutes

Scott Thomas is the guy who introduced me to competition barbecue and encouraged me to start blogging about barbecue. His backyard cuisine has been featured on TV, radio, print, and cyberspace. He's certainly a talented ambassador for the outdoor cooking scene, and Scott absolutely makes the best baby back ribs I've ever had. Note: A blowtorch is an optional piece of equipment for this recipe.

Ingredients
2 slabs baby back ribs, membrane removed

Brine
1 quart apple juice
1/4 cup table salt
2 tbsp minced garlic
1 tsp fresh cracked black pepper

Rub
2 tbsp granulated garlic
2 tbsp turbinado sugar (raw sugar)

2 tbsp pumpkin pie spice
1 tbsp sweet paprika

Glaze
2 tbsp apple jelly
2 tbsp apricot preserves
2 tbsp hot pepper jelly
2 tsp Worcestershire sauce

Instructions

1. Combine the brine ingredients in a storage bag and slosh around until the salt is dissolved.

2. Place the ribs in the bag with the brine and refrigerate overnight.

3. Combine the rub ingredients in a bowl.

4. Remove ribs from the refrigerator and give the bone side of the ribs a dusting to a coating of rub (your preference).

5. Flip the ribs and repeat on the meat side.

6. Prepare the grill for two-zone grilling (or indirect grilling) with coals and smoke wood on one side and nothing on the other.

7. Target temperature of the inside of the grill is 275 to 300 degrees F.

8. Place the ribs on the side of the grill with no heat and close the lid.

9. While the ribs are cooking, combine the glaze ingredients in a bowl and put in the microwave for about 90 seconds to liquefy the gelatin and allow the ingredients to combine. Mix well.

10. When the meat pulls back from the bone about a half-inch (about 2 hours at this temperature), flip the slabs over to the bone side and slather with the glaze.

11. If desired, blast the glaze for a couple minutes with a blowtorch (making sure the flame is blue and not orange) by constantly rocking the flame slowly back and forth across the glaze.

12. Flip over to the meat side and smear with the glaze.

13. Blast with the torch on the meat side.

14. Once a sugary crust is achieved on all the slabs, remove from the heat, allow to rest for 5 minutes, slice, and serve.

SAUSAGE KABOBS

Serves: 3

Total Time: 30 minutes

Ingredients

1 package Hillshire Farms Smoked Sausage Link

2 hot links Sausage

1 green bell pepper

1/2 large white onion

BBQ Rub (page 330)

BBQ Sauce (page 332)

Instructions

1. Set up the grill for indirect grilling.

2. Slice the sausages into 1-inch cuts.

3. Dice up the peppers and onions into 1-inch chunks.

4. Thread the peppers, onions, and sausages onto the skewers, alternating the meats and veggies.

5. Liberally sprinkle some rub on the kabobs.

6. Place the kabobs on the grill on the opposite side of the hot coals. Close the lid. The vents should be wide open on the opposite side of the hot coals.

7. Check on the kabobs after about 10 to 15 minutes. When the onions and peppers are starting to look tender, but still firm, it's time to move them over to the hot side.

8. Cook the kabobs directly over the coals until the skewers start to char a little around the edges.

9. Start applying the BBQ Sauce to the kabobs with a brush.

10. After the sauce is applied, put the kabobs back on the cool side and close the lid.

11. Kabobs are done when the veggies on the kabobs look tender.

12. Give the kabobs another coat of sauce as they come off the grill.

ARMADILLO EGGS

Serves: 4
Total Time: 2 hours

Ingredients

4 oz. Philadelphia cream cheese

2 oz. cheddar cheese, shredded

2 tbsp Tiger Sauce

4 jalapeño peppers, cored with seeds and stems
   removed

1 pound Jimmy Dean Regular Sausage

4 tsp barbecue rub

1/2 cup barbecue sauce

Instructions

1.   Prepare cream cheese filling; combine cheeses and Tiger Sauce in a bowl and mix well. Pour mix into a small storage bag to use as a pastry bag.

2.   Cut off a small notch at a corner and squeeze contents into the hollowed jalapeño peppers; set aside.

3.   Divide sausage into 1/4-pound patties and wrap each patty around a pepper. Completely cover the peppers with sausage with no creases or cracks. As a result, they are in the shape of an egg.

4.   Apply barbecue rub on the sausage-wrapped peppers.

5.   Set up the smoker at 225 degrees F. Add apple wood chunks for smoke.

6.   Cook on the smoker for 1 hours or until the sausage reaches 160 degrees F internal temperature.

7.   Paint the eggs with barbecue sauce and cook for an additional 10 minutes.

8.   Remove the eggs from the smoker and rest for 10 minutes to allow the cheese to cool down.

9.   Cut in half or serve the eggs whole.

Note:

Use any of your favorite rubs and barbecue sauces or check out ideas on page 329.

SLINGER FATTY

Serves: 8
Total Time: 2 hours, 20 minutes

Slingers are not barbecue. They are a late-night or early-morning food binge for the town drunks' enjoyment. They're only found in diners around St. Louis, but barbecue has long been the originator for curing inebriated ailments so this will fit right in.

Ingredients

1 pound pork sausage
1/4 cup canola oil
1 cup frozen hash browns
2 eggs, beaten
Kosher salt
Black pepper
1 cup chili
1/2 cup shredded cheddar cheese
1/4 cup diced onion

Instructions

1. On a sheet of plastic wrap, flatten the ground pork into a shape of a square at 1/8 of an inch thickness. Set aside.

2. Add the oil to a cast-iron skillet and cook the hash browns.

3. Once the hash browns are almost done, start prepping the eggs by adding salt and pepper and then add to the hash browns. Cook the eggs like scrambled eggs until done.

3. Pour the browns/eggs mixture directly onto the sausage.

4. Add the chili, cheese, and onion on top of the egg mixture.

5. Roll the sausage into the shape of a tube and rub the sausage to make sure you cover up any holes or crevices to prevent the filling from seeping out.

6. At this point, the fatty is too delicate to put on the grill because it is warm and mushy, so it is a good idea to firm it up a little. Wrap it with plastic wrap to hold its shape and put it in the freezer for 1 hour. It is much easier to handle when it is partially frozen.

7. Set up the grill for two-zone indirect cooking with the temperature around 375 degrees F with the air vents wide open.

8. Place the fatty on the cool side of the grill and put the lid on.

9. If you want a smoky flavor, you can add a chunk of peach wood for smoke.

10. Cook the fatty for 2 hours.

11. Remove from the cooker when the internal temperature reaches 165 degrees F.

12. Rest for 15 minutes, slice, and serve.

SICILIAN PORK CHOPS

Serves: 2

Total Time: 30 minutes + brining time

Ingredients

2 1-inch-thick pork chops

Canola oil spray

Salt and pepper

1/2 lb Cooked Spaghetti pasta

Pork Brine Ingredients

8 cups ice-cold water

1/2 cup Kosher salt

1/4 cup sugar

2 tbsp unsulfured molasses

1 tbsp red pepper flakes

1 tbsp dried thyme leaves

Sicilian Breadcrumbs

1 cup breadcrumbs

2 tbsp dry pesto seasoning

2 tbsp grated pecorino Romano cheese

Garnish

1 Roma tomato, sliced and grilled

1 tsp grated pecorino Romano cheese

Chopped Italian parsley

Cracked black peppercorns

Pork Brine Instructions

1.   Turn on stove to medium-high heat.

2.   In a large saucepan, combine 2 cups of water with the salt and sugar. Start heating the brine.

3.   Stir continuously until the sugar and salt are dissolved. Take the brine off the heat and let it cool.

4.   Pour the remaining water, molasses, red pepper flakes, and thyme leaves into a large container that has a lid.

5.   Add the brine to the large container and mix well.

6.   Add the pork chops to the brine and place in the refrigerator overnight.

Cooking Instructions

1.   Prepare the grill with the 2-zone setup at 350 degrees. Combine Sicilian Breadcrumbs ingredients in food processor and mix well.

2.   Remove the chops from the brine, rinse, and dry.

3.   Salt and pepper the pork chops.

4.   Coat pork chops with the Sicilian Breadcrumbs.

5.   Place chops directly over the heat on an elevated wire rack.

6.   Cook with the lid on until both sides show a light char (approximately 4 minutes on each side). The internal temperature should reach 140 degrees F. If the temperature is too low when the surface is charred, move to the cool side of the grill, cover lid, and indirect cook until done.

7.   Serve on plate of pasta.

8.   Garnish with grilled tomato slices, more cheese, parsley, and fresh cracked pepper.

PORK CHOPS & PEACHES

Serves: 2
Total Time: 30 minutes

Ingredients

2 1-inch thick pork rib chops
Vegetable oil
Salt and pepper
2 tbsp unsalted butter
1/4 cup sugar
2 peaches, firm and sliced

Cider Brine Ingredients

2 cups apple juice
2 cups water
1/3 cup Kosher salt
1/3 cup brown sugar
2 tbsp red pepper flakes
1/2 tsp ground cinnamon

Cider Brine Instructions

1. In a saucepan, bring apple juice, water, salt, and brown sugar to a boil, stirring regularly.

Instructions

1. Set grill to indirect heat, 350 degrees F.
2. Remove chops from the brine and pat dry excess brine.
3. Coat chops in vegetable oil and season with salt and pepper.
4. Place chops on the cool side of the grill and cover the grill with the lid, top vents wide open.
5. When the chops reach an internal temperature of 135 degrees F, remove the grill lid and let the fire build to over 500 degrees F.
6. Directly grill the pork chops over the fire until you start to see char marks.
7. Remove from the grill once internal temperature reaches 140 degrees.
8. Let the chops rest on a plate for 5 minutes loosely covered with foil before serving.
9. Meanwhile, in a skillet over direct heat on the grill or on a range at medium heat, melt butter and add sugar. Mix well.
10. Add sliced peaches. Cook until peaches are brown and the sauce thickens.
11. Serve pork chops topped with sautéed peaches and sauce.

COLE'S SWEET HEAT RIBS

Cole's Sweet Heat BBQ Sauce
Cole Harte
www.colessweetheat.com

Ingredients
1 rack St. Louis ribs, trimmed
Basic Rib Rub (see below)
Cole's Sweet Heat BBQ Sauce

Basic Rib Rub Ingredients
1/2 cup dark brown sugar
1/4 cup paprika
1/8 cup salt
1 tbsp black pepper
2 tbsp hot chili powder
1 tbsp garlic powder
1 tbsp onion powder
1 tsp cayenne pepper
1 tsp cinnamon

Foil Wrap
1 stick unsalted butter
1/4 cup brown sugar
1/4 cup Sriracha sauce
1/8 cup light corn syrup

Instructions
1. Combine all Basic Rib Rub ingredients in a bowl and mix well. Season the ribs with the rub.
2. Smoke the ribs at 250 degrees F for 2 hours.
3. Wrap the ribs in foil with all the wrap ingredients and return to the smoker for 1 hour.
4. Unwrap the foil and apply Cole's Sweet Heat BBQ Sauce.
5. Place the ribs back on smoker for 1/2 hour.
6. Slice into bones and serve immediately.

Notes:
1. Apply the two-zone indirect heat set up if no smoker is available.
2. Use enough foil to wrap completely around the ribs. I recommend using 2 sheets for durability.
3. Add chunks of smoke wood such as apple, cherry, or peach.
4. Essentially, this applies a 2-1-1 method. See the 3-2-1 method on page 13.

JEFF'S ST. LOUIS-STYLE RIBS

Phatso's BBQ
Jeff Fitter
Catering Company and BBQ Competition Team
www.phatsosbbq.com

Serves: 9
Total Time: 5 hours

Ingredients
3 racks spareribs, trimmed
Jeff's St. Louis-style Rub (see below)
Barbecue sauce (optional)
Cherry wood
Pecan wood

Jeff's St. Louis-style Rub Ingredients
1 cup brown sugar
1 cup white sugar
1/3 cup celery salt
1/3 cup black pepper
1/3 cup garlic powder
1/3 cup dry mustard
1/3 cup onion powder
1 tbsp cayenne pepper

Jeff's St. Louis-Style Rub Instructions Cooking Instructions

1. Trim the rib up a little. Remove any large chunks of meat and if needed (due to space limits or if it just looks bad) remove the last few ribs on either end. Be sure to cook them (see Rib Tips with Honey-Grapefruit Glaze, page 112).

2. Mix all rub ingredients together in a bowl. Apply the rub on the back side of the rib, just enough to see it's there. The back side needs flavor too! Now flip the rib over and apply the rub to the rib. I like to rub that in and make sure the meat is covered completely before moving on.

3. Repeat step 2 until all ribs are rubbed. Then leave the ribs on a tray or wrapped and store them in the refrigerator or cooler for not more than 12 hours but at least 3 hours to let that flavor settle in.

4. Bring smoker up to 250 degrees F and add cherry or apple wood for smoke .

5. Place the ribs on the smoker and close the lid (or door). Remember, if you're looking, they ain't cooking!

6. Cook time may vary (depending on the smoker used). To determine when the rib is ready to serve, use a set of tongs to pick the rib up a long way from the end, at about the middle of the rib. The rib should bend to the point of nearly making a frown and you will see the meat pulling but not tearing apart.

7.   If desired, sauce the ribs before serving. I prefer to leave my ribs dry and let each person determine if they wish to sauce it; everyone in my family is different!

Notes:

1.   If a smoker is not available, use the two-zone indirect heat method. Use wood chunks for this setup.

2.   Trimming ribs is discussed on page 9.

3.   Other methods for checking doneness for ribs can be found on page 13.

4.   Find a BBQ Sauce recipe on page 332.

PULLED PORK EGG ROLLS

Serves: 8
Total Time: 1 1/2 hours

Ingredients

1 tbsp canola oil (more for deep frying)
1/2 napa cabbage
2 stalks celery, julienne
3 stalks green onion, rough chop (white parts too)
16 egg roll wraps
1/2 pound pulled pork, smoked
2 tbsp cornstarch
1 tbsp water
Kosher salt
Black pepper

Gravy

2 tbsp soy sauce
1/2 tbsp rice vinegar
1/2 tsp bonito flakes, crushed (optional)

Dipping Sauce

2 tbsp hoisin sauce
1/2 tbsp garlic, minced
1 tsp honey
1 tsp soy sauce

Instructions

1. Setup deep fryer at 375 degrees F.
2. Prepare cabbage mix: in a skillet on medium heat add oil, cabbage, celery, and onions. Sauté for a few minutes, then add gravy ingredients. Cook until vegetables are soft, then drain excess liquids. Let cool and set aside.
3. Using 2 layers at a time, lay egg roll wraps in the shape of a diamond. Add 1/3 cup of pork and 1/4 cup of cabbage mixture in the center of the wrap.
4. Roll the nearest point over the pork, fold the sides inwards, then roll the top point over tightly so it forms a cylinder.
5. Prepare paste: mix cornstarch and water together.
6. Seal edges of roll with paste; apply with finger under the edges.
7. Deep fry the rolls in small batches for 3 minutes or until wrap is crispy and light brown in color.
8. Prepare dipping sauce: in saucepan on medium-low heat, combine and stir all dipping sauce ingredients. Cook until the sauce is warm.
9. Serve rolls with dipping sauce.

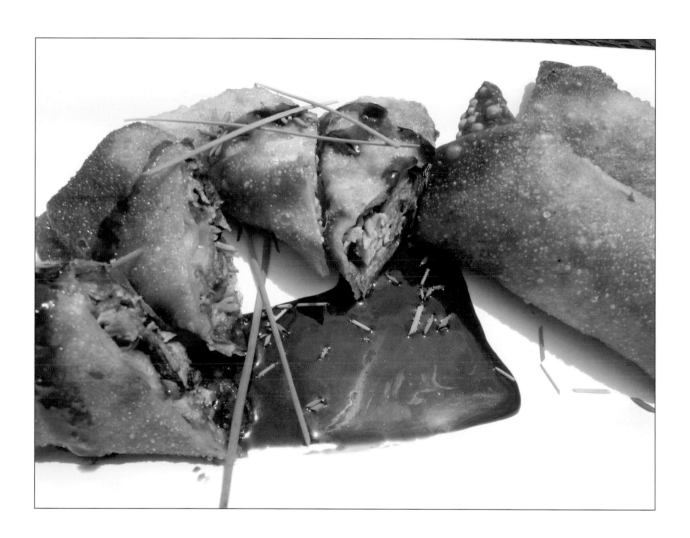

SMOKED BRATWURST GYRO

Serves: 8
Total Time: 1 hours

Ingredients

8 bratwursts
3 12-oz. cans light beer
1 large yellow onion, sliced
4 cloves garlic, crushed
Code 3 Spices Rescue Rub
8 Kangaroo Traditional White Flatbread
4 oz. lettuce, shredded
1 medium tomato, diced
Tzatziki Sauce (see below)

Tzatziki Sauce Ingredients

3 tbsp olive oil
1 tbsp apple cider vinegar
2 cloves garlic, minced finely
1/2 tsp salt
1/4 tsp white pepper
1 shallot, chopped
1/4 tsp cayenne pepper
1 tsp pepper sauce
1 tbsp Greek seasoning
1 cup Greek yogurt, strained
1 cup sour cream
1 cucumber, peeled, seeded, and diced
1 tsp chopped fresh dill

Tzatziki Sauce Instructions

1. Combine olive oil, vinegar, garlic, salt, pepper, shallot, cayenne pepper, pepper sauce, and Greek seasoning in a food processor. Mix until well combined.

2. Using a whisk, blend the yogurt with the sour cream.

3. Add the olive oil mixture to the yogurt mixture and mix well.

4. Add the cucumber and chopped fresh dill.

5. Chill for at least 2 hours before serving.

6. Garnish with a sprig of fresh dill just before serving.

Cooking Instructions

1. Set up the cooker for direct grilling at 350 degrees F.

2. In a foil pan, combine the brats, beer, onions, garlic, and 1 tbsp of barbecue rub. Cover and seal with a sheet of aluminum foil. Cook for 1 hour directly over the heat with the lid on the cooker.

3. Make the Tzatziki Sauce.

4. When the brats reach an internal temperature of 165 degrees F, they are done. Remove the brats and warm the flatbread over direct heat.

5. On a flatbread, layer a brat, lettuce, tomato, and Tzatziki Sauce, and dust with rub on top.

6. Serve immediately.

PORK TENDERLOIN SLIDER

Lock, Stock and Two Smokin' Barrels (Bill
     Grenko)
Competition BBQ Team
www.lsatsb.blogspot.ca

Serves: 12
Total Time: 1 1/2 hours

Ingredients

1-pound pork tenderloin
2 tbsp prepared yellow mustard
2 tbsp Code 3 Rescue Rub
1/2 cup mayonnaise
1/2 cup Blues Hog Tennessee Red Sauce
12 slider buns
Famous Dave's Spicy Pickle Chips

Instructions

1.   Slather pork tenderloin with yellow mustard.

2.   Lightly season with Rescue Rub.

3.   Smoke at 300 degrees F until pork reaches an internal temperature of 140 to 145 degrees F.

4.   Remove from smoker, wrap with aluminum foil, and rest for 30 minutes.

5.   Slice tenderloin into 1/2-inch-thick disks.

6.   Mix mayonnaise and Blues Hog Tennessee Red Sauce.

7.   Place pork on bun, spread on sauce mixture, and top with pickles.

CANDIED BACON

Serves: 2–4
Total Time: 40 minutes

My LDL levels just spiked because I read this recipe. Here's another popular barbecue treat with a cult following, with my own twist.

Ingredients

6 strips bacon, thick cut
1/3 cup Mexican brown sugar (piloncillo)
1 tbsp chile de arbol, ground

Instructions

1. Setup cooker for indirect heat at 400 degrees F.
2. In a half-size deep foil pan with a cooling rack inside, place bacon side by side.
3. Evenly apply brown sugar over the bacon, then sprinkle the ground chile pepper on top.
4. Cook for 20 to 30 minutes until bacon is done and the sugar has caramelized.
5. Serve immediately.

Notes:

1. If desired, substitute regular brown sugar for the Mexican version.
2. Piloncillo is shaped like a cone and it is hard as a rock. Heat it in the microwave for 15 to 30 seconds at a time to soften up. Alternatively, you can use a cheese grater to shave the cone down.

ATOMIC APPLE RIBS

Serves: 3
Total Time: 5 hours

Ingredients
1 rack pork St. Louis-style sparerib, trimmed
2 tbsp canola oil
Apple Rub (see below)
2 cups apple juice, spray bottle
Hot Cinnamon BBQ Sauce (see below)

Apple Rub Ingredients
2 tbsp brown sugar
1 tbsp Hungarian paprika
1 tsp apple pie spice
1/2 tsp garlic powder
1/2 tsp onion powder
Black pepper
Kosher salt

Foil Wrap
2 cups brown sugar
1 cup apple jelly
1/2 cup Parkay Squeeze

Hot Cinnamon BBQ Sauce Ingredients
1/4 cup orange juice
1/2 cup Red Hots candy
1 1/2 cups ketchup
3 tbsp Worcestershire sauce
2 tbsp molasses
2 tsp Granny Smith apples, finely minced
1 tsp garlic, finely minced
1/2 tsp Hungarian paprika
1/4 tsp red pepper flakes

Hot Cinnamon BBQ Sauce Instructions
1.   In a saucepan on medium heat, combine the orange juice and candy. Put the lid on and cook until the candy is melted down.

2.   Add all remaining ingredients into the saucepan, then mix well and reduce the heat to a simmer for 15 minutes. Sauce is done when it thickens.

3.   Let the sauce cool and store it in a glass jar. Refrigerate until ready to use.

Cooking Instructions
1.   Set up smoker at 225 degrees F. Add apple wood chunks for smoke.

2.   Combine all Apple Rub ingredients and mix well in a bowl. Coat ribs with oil and apply the rub. Let the rubbed ribs sit at room temperature until the rub becomes a syrup glaze.

3.   Smoke ribs on the smoker for 2 hours, spraying ribs with apple juice after the first hour and in 30-minute intervals thereafter.

4.   Get 2 sheets of aluminum foil (enough to wrap the ribs) and place half of the wrap ingredients in the center. Place the ribs meat side down on the sugar, jelly, and butter mixture and top the ribs off with the other half. Wrap the

ribs tightly in the foil and cook on the smoker for 2 hours.

5.   Check for doneness and remove from the smoker.

6.   Unwrap the foil and turn the ribs meat side up. Return the ribs in the opened foil to the smoker for 30 minutes to cook in their own juices.

7.   In the last 10 minutes, apply Hot Cinnamon BBQ Sauce.

8.   Remove the ribs from the smoker and rest for 10 minutes.

9.   Slice into individual bones and serve immediately.

Note:

Essentially, this is applying a 2-2-0.5 method for smoking ribs (See 3-2-1 method on page 13).

CIDER BRINED BBQ PORK LOIN

Serves: 6–8

Total Time: 2 hours + brining time

Ingredients

3-pound pork loin, boneless
Cider Brine (see below)
MLG Rib Rub (see below)
2 tbsp canola oil

Cider Brine Ingredients

2 cups apple cider
2 cups water
1/3 cup Kosher salt
1/3 cup brown sugar
2 tbsp red pepper flakes
1/2 tsp ground cinnamon

MLG Rib Rub Ingredients

1/2 cup turbinado sugar
3 tbsp Kosher salt
1 tbsp garlic powder
1 tbsp onion powder
1 tbsp chili powder
1 tbsp Hungarian paprika
1 tbsp black pepper
1/2 tsp cayenne pepper

Cider Brine Instructions

1. In a saucepan, bring all brine ingredients (except the red pepper flakes) to a boil, stirring regularly.

2. When all is dissolved, take saucepan off heat and let the brine cool.

3. Add red pepper flakes into a large container that has a lid.

4. Add the brine to the large container and mix well.

Instructions

1. Prepare the pork loin by trimming off most of the fat cap, but leave a thin amount on the loin. Any silver skin must be removed too.

2. In a 1-gallon storage bag, combine the brine and pork loin. Refrigerate overnight.

3. Set up the smoker using indirect heat at 250 degrees F. Add apple wood chunks for smoke.

4. Combine all MLG Rib Rub ingredients in a bowl and mix well. Coat the pork loin with oil and lightly season with the rub.

5. Place the loin on the smoker and cook for 1 1/2 hours or until the internal temperature reaches 140 degrees F.

6. Remove from the cooker and rest for 10 minutes or until the loin is cool enough to handle.

7. Slice and serve.

CHAPTER 4

YARDBIRD RECIPES

TURKEY DAY SMOKED TURKEY

Serves: 10

Total Time: 5 hours + 36-hour brine

Ingredients

15-pound whole fresh turkey, innards removed

2 tbsp canola oil

1 oz. fresh herbs (thyme, rosemary, and sage)

2 sticks unsalted butter

6 cloves garlic, minced

Turkey Brine

1 gallon water, cold

1 cup Kosher salt

1 cup white sugar

1 oz. fresh herbs (thyme, rosemary, and sage)

2 bay leaves

1 lemon, halved

1 tbsp black peppercorns

5 cloves garlic, crushed

1 medium yellow onion, chopped

Turkey Rub

1 tbsp garlic salt

1 tbsp onion powder

1/2 tbsp chili powder

1/2 tbsp paprika

1/4 tbsp black pepper

Instructions

1. In a saucepan, dissolve the salt and sugar for the brine in 5 cups of boiling water. Let the solution cool.

2. Add the salt and sugar solution and all remaining brine ingredients into a container or cooler lined with a plastic bag, big enough to immerse the bird. Add the turkey and shake up the container to evenly distribute all the ingredients.

3. Brine the turkey in the refrigerator or a cooler full of ice for 36 hours.

4. Make the rub by combining all the rub ingredients in a bowl and mix well.

5. Set up the smoker at 275 degrees F. Add apple wood chunks for smoke.

6. Remove the turkey from the brine and place it in a foil pan large enough for it. Wipe off excess brine with paper towels.

7. Coat the bird with oil and apply the rub all over, including inside the cavity. Place the herbs in the cavity for aromatics.

8. Place the foil pan in the pit and smoke for 1 hour.

9. In a saucepan, melt the butter and add the garlic. Simmer until the garlic is soft.

10. Check the turkey for color. When the skin is starting to brown, baste the turkey with the melted butter and cover with a sheet of aluminum foil. Cook for 2 more hours, basting once after the first hour.

11. Remove the foil and cook for 1 hour, basting the bird every 30 minutes or until the bird is done at 160 degrees F internal temperature in the dark meat.

12. When the turkey is done, remove from the smoker and rest at room temperature for 30 minutes or until cool enough to handle. Give a final brush of melted butter.

13. Slice the turkey and serve.

HABANERO ISLAND CHICKEN

Serves: 6
Total Time: 2 1/2 hours + marinating

Ingredients

1 whole chicken, fresh
1 white onion
8 cloves garlic, crushed
6 habanero peppers, deseeded and chopped
8 scallions, chopped
2 oz. fresh ginger root, chopped
2 tbsp thyme
2 tsp cinnamon
2 tbsp allspice
2 tbsp Kosher salt
1/2 cup soy sauce
2 tbsp white sugar
1/2 cup canola oil
2 tsp black pepper
2 tsp nutmeg
1/2 tsp cloves
1 cup bitter orange juice
1 cup white vinegar

Instructions

1. Prepare marinade: combine all ingredients (except the chicken) in a food processor and mix well. Pour marinade into a 2-gallon storage bag.

2. Spatchcock the chicken (see page 17).

3. Place the chicken in the marinade and refrigerate for 24 hours.

4. Set up cooker for indirect heat cooking at 250 degrees F.

5. Remove chicken from the marinade and wipe off excess with paper towels.

6. Place chicken on the grill, skin down, and cook for 2 hours.

7. Chicken is done with the dark meat reaches 160 degrees F.

8. Cut the bird into thighs, legs, breasts, and wings.

9. Serve immediately.

Note:

For more flavor, add allspice berries and cinnamon sticks to the fire to create scented smoke.

ASIAN GRILLED CHICKEN THIGHS

Chef Todd Kussman

Serves: 6–8
Total Time: 50 minutes + marinating

Ingredients

1/2 cup honey

1/2 cup freshly squeezed or canned Mandarin
    orange juice

1/2 cup soy sauce

1/4 cup sesame oil

1/4 cup rice wine vinegar

2 tbsp fresh grated ginger

1 tsp red pepper flake

1 tsp garlic powder

Salt and pepper to taste

6–8 chicken thighs, skin on

Instructions

1. Place chicken thighs in a resealable storage bag.

2. Combine all remaining liquid and dry ingredients in the storage bag. Place in the refrigerator to marinate 1 to 4 hours.

3. Prepare the grill for indirect heat cooking with the lid off for searing at 500+ degrees F. Remove chicken thighs from marinade and place skin side down over hot, glowing charcoal or medium-high gas grill.

4. Grill for approximately 2 minutes or long enough to get defined grill marks and good color on skin side (with any marinade containing high sugar content, be careful not to burn).

5. Turn and grill for another 2 minutes.

6. Once both sides have been high-heat grilled, move thighs to an indirectly heated portion of the grill and continue to cook with cover on until their internal temperature reaches 145 to 155 degrees F. The wings should continue to increase in temperature by another 3 to 5 degrees F once you remove them from the grill.

3-HERB ROASTED CHICKEN

Serves: 4

Total Time: 3 hours

Ingredients

1 whole fresh chicken

1 tbsp thyme leaves, dried

1 tbsp rosemary leaves, dried

1 tbsp oregano leaves, dried

1 tsp cumin

1 tsp onion powder

1 tsp black pepper

1/2 tbsp garlic salt

1/2 tsp white pepper

2 tbsp vegetable oil

Instructions

1.   Set up cooker for indirect heat cooking at 250 degrees F. Add chunks of oakwood for smoke.

2.   Combine the thyme, rosemary and oregano and grind them in a spice grinder.

3.   Combine thyme, rosemary, oregano, cumin, onion powder, black pepper, garlic salt and white pepper in a small bowl.

4.   Spatchcock the chicken (see page 17).

5.   Dry chicken off with paper towels.

6.   Apply vegetable oil on bone side first and then dust with dry rub. Repeat on skin side.

7.   Place chicken on the cool side of the grill, skin side down, and cook for 2 hours.

8.   Chicken is done when the dark meat reaches 165 degrees F.

9.   Cut the bird into thighs, legs, breasts, and wings.

10. Serve immediately.

HULI HULI CHICKEN

Serves: 4
Total Time: 1 hour + marinating

Ingredients

4 chicken quarters

1/4 cup soy sauce

1 tbsp sherry cooking wine

1/2 tsp Worcestershire sauce

1/4 cup ketchup

1 tbsp minced garlic

1" fresh ginger, peeled and minced

1/2 cup crushed pineapple

1/4 cup brown sugar

Instructions

1.   Combine all the ingredients except the chicken together in a bowl. Mix with a whisk.

2.   Place the chicken in a 1-gallon storage bag. Pour the marinade in with the chicken and seal the storage bag.

3.   Refrigerate the marinating chicken overnight.

4.   Set up the grill for indirect cooking at 375 degrees F.

5.   Place the chicken on the cool side of the grill.

6.   Add a pile of mesquite wood chips or chunks on tip of the grill grate and let them smolder and infuse the chicken for a more authentic tasting Huli Huli Chicken.

7.   Place the lid on the grill and cook for 45 minutes before checking it again. Make sure the vents are wide open and over the food.

8.   Chicken is done after 45 minutes.

9.   Remove and enjoy!

SKINLESS SMOKED TURKEY BREAST

Serves: 4–6
Total Time: 3 hours

Ingredients

6-pound turkey breast, whole
2 tbsp MLG Poultry Rub (see below)
2 tbsp canola oil
2 cups beef broth

MLG Poultry Rub

1 tbsp garlic salt
1 tbsp onion powder
1/2 tbsp chili powder
1/2 tbsp paprika
1/4 tbsp black pepper

Cooking Instructions

1. Set up smoker for 250 degrees F.
2. Make the rub by combining all the rub ingredients in a bowl and mix well. Remove skin from turkey breast, coat with oil, and apply dry rub.
3. Place turkey in a foil pan and smoke for 1 hour.
4. Add beef broth and cover pan with a sheet of foil for 2 hours.
5. When the internal temperature of the breast reaches 155 degrees F, it's done.
6. Remove from grill and let it cool for 30 minutes, under loose foil, until it's cool enough to handle.
7. Serve immediately.

Notes:

1. Use a brine to add moisture and flavor. I suggest the poultry brine on page 338.
2. Any fruit wood, hickory, pecan, or oak wood adds great smoke flavor.
3. Refrigerate after cooking. This recipe is great for leftovers (see page 302).

MAPLE BOURBON CHICKEN LEG QUARTERS

Serves: 6
Total time: 1 hour

Ingredients

6 chicken leg quarters
1 cup Sweet Baby Rays original barbecue sauce
1 cup maple syrup
1/4 cup bourbon
1 tbsp bacon fat
2 tbsp apple cider vinegar
1 tbsp mustard powder
1/2 tsp onion powder
1/2 tsp garlic powder
1 tsp smoked paprika (or Hungarian paprika)
1 tbsp red pepper flakes
Salt and pepper to taste
2 tbsp MLG Poultry Rub

Instructions

1. Set up the cooker for indirect heat cooking at 250 degrees F. Add chunks of apple wood for smoke.

2. Apply the poultry rub all over the chicken thighs.

3. Place the chicken pieces on the cool side of the grill away from the heat and put the lid on the cooker with the vents wide open. Cook for 50 minutes until the internal temperature reaches 145 degrees F.

4. In a medium saucepan, warm the remaining ingredients on medium heat until the sauce starts to simmer, then turn off the heat and let it cool.

5. Use a basting brush to apply the sauce on all the thighs. Cook for 10 minutes or until the internal temperature reaches 160 degrees F.

6. Apply more sauce on the chicken pieces and serve immediately.

4-LAYER BARBECUED GAME HENS

Patio Daddio BBQ
John Dawson
BBQ Blogger
www.patiodaddiobbq.com

Serves: 2
Total Time: 1 1/2 hours + brining time

Ingredients

2 Cornish game hens (24 oz.), thawed and rinsed
  with giblets removed
2 cups hot water
1/3 cup Kosher salt
3 cups ice
1 can (12 oz.) apricot nectar
2 Tbsp Grill Mates Montreal Chicken Seasoning
2 Tbsp Grill Mates Sweet & Smoky Rub
Canola oil cooking spray
2 small cans (5.5 oz.) apple juice
1/2 cup your favorite barbecue sauce

Instructions

1. Combine the hot water and salt in a large bowl and stir until the salt is dissolved.

2. Add the ice, nectar, and Montreal Chicken Seasoning to the bowl and mix well.

3. Add the hens to the brine, cover, and refrigerate 6 hours. Note: Make sure that the birds are completely submerged.

4. Once the hens are done brining, remove them from the liquid, drain them completely, and pat them dry with paper towels.

5. Prepare your grill for indirect cooking at medium heat (about 375 degrees F).

6. Coat each hen liberally (including the cavity) with the rub.

7. Coat the skin of each hen with the cooking oil spray.

8. Open the cans of juice and pour out about half.

9. Insert the open end of a can into each hen cavity.

10. Set the cans with the birds upright on the grill away from the direct heat.

11. Grill the hens indirect for 1 hour and 15 minutes, or until they reach an internal temperature of 170 degrees F in the thigh.

12. Remove the can from each bird, return the birds to the grill, and coat each liberally with barbecue sauce.

13. Continue cooking the hens 5 more minutes.

14. Split the hens in half, serve, and enjoy!

GRILLED CHICKEN SALAD FILLED ENDIVE

Chef Todd Kussman

Serving Size: 4
Total Time: 30 minutes

Ingredients

4 chicken breasts, seasoned with your favorite
    rub
1 1/2 cups mayonnaise
1/2 cups Dijon mustard
1 cup pickle relish
1 tsp curry powder
5–6 green onions, sliced thin
2 hard boiled eggs, diced
Salt and pepper to taste
6–8 bulbs of Belgian endive, base cut and outer
    leaves peeled away

Instructions

1.   Grill seasoned chicken breasts over medium-high heat.

2.   Remove when breasts reach 150 to 160 degrees F and place in refrigerator to cool.

3.   Combine mayonnaise, mustard, relish, and curry powder.

4.   When chicken breasts are fully cooled, cut into small dice.

5.   Fold diced chicken breasts, green onions, and diced egg into the mayonnaise mixture.

6.   Season with salt and pepper if desired and serve in Belgian endive leaves. Also goes well served in dollar rolls or as a tortilla wrap.

BEER CAN CHICKEN

Code 3 Spices (Chris Bohnemeier)
BBQ Rub Company
www.code3spices.com

Serves: 6
Total Time: 1 hour, 50 minutes

Beer can chicken is probably the easiest of recipes, but turns out great flavors every time. The key to beer can chicken is to make sure that the skin turns out crispy.

Ingredients
2 whole frying chickens
2 cans of beer
2 tbsp vegetable oil
6 tbsp Code 3 Spices 5-0 Rub

Instructions
1.   Remove neck and giblets from chicken and discard. Rinse chicken inside and out, and pat dry with paper towel. Apply the oil all over the chicken skin and then rub the bird with Code 3 Spices 5-0 Rub.

2.   Open beer cans and empty half of each can (you choose how).

3.   Firmly grab chicken and place cavity over top of beer can. Place the beer can chicken on the grill and use the legs to create a tripod to balance the chicken.

4.   Cook the chicken over medium-high indirect heat with the lid on for 1 hours.

5.   The chicken is done when the breast reaches 165 degrees F and the thigh is 180 degrees F.

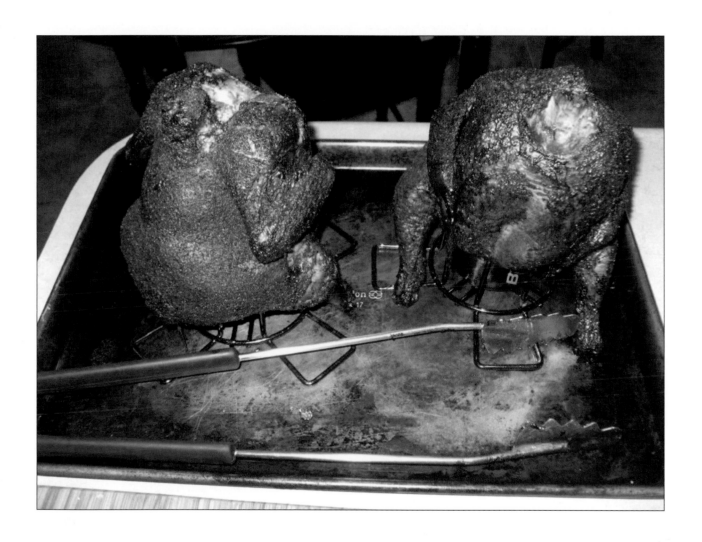

BLAZIN' SMOKED CHICKEN CHALLENGE

Serves: 1–2
Total Time: 1 hour, 10 minutes

Here is a challenge for you: make this recipe and see if you can stand the heat! I admit, I could not do it, but the half bite I took tasted really good. No use of extracts—it's all about the peppers with a lot of flavor to be found in this spicy treat.

Ingredients
1 pound chicken wing pieces

Caliente Rub
1 tbsp brown sugar
1 tbsp smoky paprika
1/2 tbsp Kosher salt
1/2 tbsp coarse black pepper
1/2 tsp cayenne pepper
1/2 tsp chili powder
1/2 tsp white pepper
1/2 tsp chile de arbol, ground (optional)
1/2 tsp guajillo dried peppers, ground (optional)

Caliente Sauce
2 cups ketchup
2 cups Valentina's black label hot sauce (or use Frank's)
1/2 cup water
1/3 cup tequila
1/3 cup brown sugar
2 tbsp Dijon mustard
1 tbsp onion powder
1 tbsp garlic powder
1/2 tsp cayenne pepper
1/2 tsp chile de arbol, ground (optional)
1/2 tsp guajillo dried peppers, ground (optional)

Instructions

1. Mix all rub ingredients in a bowl and set aside.
2. Whisk all sauce ingredients in a small pot to put on the grill.
3. Set up grill for a two-zone indirect grilling, add chunks of fruit wood.
4. Apply the rub on the chicken wings.
5. Place wings on the cool side of the grill with the lid on.
6. Place sauce on cool side of the grill to absorb the smoky scent.
7. Cook the chicken for 40 minutes at 325 to 350 degrees F. Don't flip the wings.
8. Dip the wings in the sauce, place back on the grill, cook for 10 minutes more. Repeat dipping and cooking once more.
9. Remove from grill and serve.

LSTSB CHICKEN WINGS

Lock, Stock and Two Smokin' Barrels (Bill
    Grenko)
Competition BBQ Team
www.lsatsb.blogspot.ca

Serves: 3
Total Time: 1 1/2 hours + brining time

Ingredients

3 pounds whole chicken wings
1/2 cup Kosher salt
1/2 cup white sugar
2 quarts water
2 tbsp garlic powder
1 tbsp ground black pepper
Canola oil
Code 3 Backdraft Rub

Instructions

1.   Start brine by dissolving Kosher salt and sugar in water.

2.   Add garlic powder and black pepper to brine and stir well.

3.   Place chicken in a large resealable storage bag and pour in brine.

4.   Seal bag, removing as much air as possible.

5.   Place bag in a plastic container (in case of leak) and refrigerate for 4–6 hours.

6.   Remove chicken from brine and pat dry with a paper towel.

7.   Lightly oil chicken and sprinkle with Backdraft rub. Caution: Rub is very spicy, so go light to avoid the heat.

8.   Smoke at 300 degrees F until skin is brown and crispy and the temperature in the drumstick portion is at least 175 degrees F.

STICKY HOISIN APRICOT CHICKEN THIGHS

Serves: 6
Total time: 1 hour 10 minutes

Ingredients

6 chicken thighs, bone-in and skin on

3/4 cup Hoisin sauce

1/2 cup apricot preserves

1 tbsp Sriracha sauce

1 tbsp Dijon mustard

2 tbsp all-purpose grilling rub

Instructions

1. Set up the cooker for indirect heat cooking at 375 degrees F. Add chunks of peach wood for smoke.

2. Apply the rub all over the chicken thighs.

3. Place the thighs on the cool side of the grill away from the heat and put the lid on the cooker with the vents wide open. Cook for 30 minutes.

4. In a medium saucepan, warm the remaining ingredients on medium heat until the sauce starts to simmer, then turn off the heat and let it cool.

5. Use a basting brush to apply the sauce on all the thighs. Cook for 10 minutes.

6. With the lid off, grill the thighs directly over the heat until a char starts to develop, then move the thighs back to cool side of the grill and put the lid back on. Cook for 10 minutes.

7. Repeat step 6.

8 Chicken thighs are done when the internal temperature reaches 160 degrees F.

9. Serve immediately.

BIG AL'S SUPER CHICKEN WINGS WITH SUPER SAUCE

Canadian Bakin' (Al Bowman)
Competition BBQ Team

Serves: 5
Total Time: 1 hour

Ingredients
5 pounds chicken wings
1/2 cup Code 3 Rescue Rub

Super Sauce Ingredients
1 bottle Durkee's Famous Sauce
1/2 cup Frank's Red Hot
1/2 stick butter, melted

Instructions

1. Mix all sauce ingredients and set aside.
2. Separate wings into: wing tips, drumettes, and mid joint which make up all 3 parts of a chicken wing. Discard tips.
3. Lightly sprinkle Rescue Rub over wings to coat.
4. Smoke or grill wings at 350 degrees F, using fruit wood such as Mojobricks cherry until juices run clear, about 45 minutes.
5. Toss cooked wings in Super Sauce. Serve immediately.

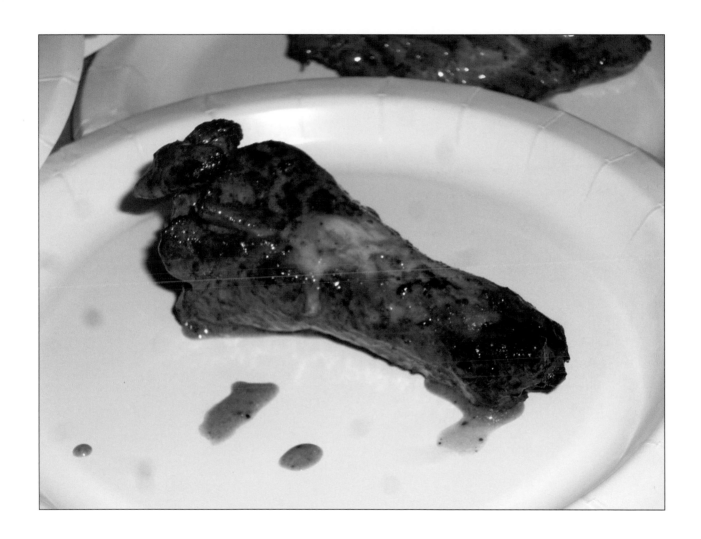

SMOKED TURKEY SALAD SANDWICH

Serves: 4

Total Time: 10 minutes

Ingredients

1 pound smoked turkey, diced

1/2 cup mayonnaise

1 oz. celery, chopped

1/2 medium green apple, diced (core removed)

1 oz. pomegranate seeds

2 slices cooked bacon, chopped

1 shallot, chopped

1/2 tsp Kosher salt

1/2 tsp black pepper

1 loaf whole-grain artisan bread

Instructions

1. In a large bowl, combine all ingredients (except the bread) and mix well.

2. Cut the loaf of bread into 8 slices to make 4 sandwiches.

3. Divide the turkey salad into 4 evenly measured scoops and place one on each sandwich.

4. Serve immediately.

CHAPTER 5

MEXI-QUE RECIPES

TACOS AL PASTOR

Serves: 5
Total Time: 6 hours 25 minutes

Ingredients
4-pound boneless Boston butt, trimmed
Yellow mustard
1 medium onion

Marinade Ingredients
4 cups pureed guajillo chiles
2 cups crushed pineapple
2 chipotle peppers in adobo sauce
2 cloves of garlic
2 tbsp white wine sherry

Rub Ingredients
4 tbsp cumin
4 tbsp oregano
1 tsp jalapeño powder
1 tsp smoked paprika
1 tsp white pepper
1 tsp black pepper
1 tsp salt

To Serve
Onion, diced
Cilantro
Radishes, sliced
Corn tortillas

Instructions
1. Slather pork with mustard.
2. Place pork in resealable storage bag, refrigerate, and marinate overnight.
3. Prepare the rub by combining rub ingredients in a bowl. Wipe mustard off pork with paper towels and apply dry rub (reserving at least 2 tbsp for the marinade).
4. Set up smoker or indirect heat grill for 250 degrees F with apple wood. Cook the pork until it reaches 160 degrees internal temperature.
5. Blend the marinade ingredients and the reserved rub in a blender until smooth.
6. Pour the marinade through a mesh colander to filter out large particles.
7. Slice the onion and place it in the bottom of a foil pan.
8. When pork reaches 160 degrees internal temperature, place it in foil pan.
9. Pour the marinade over the pork.
10. Cover the foil pan with a sheet of foil.
11. Increase grill temperature to 350 degrees F. Place foil pan on the grill.
12. Cook the pork until it reaches 190 degrees F internal temperature, or until tender.
13. Remove pork from the grill and let it rest for at least 30 minutes or until it's cool enough to handle.
14. Pull pork into chunks, and mix well with the marinade.
15. Serve with diced onion, cilantro, and sliced radishes on doubled layered corn tortillas with cerveza to wash it down.

CARNE ASADA

Serves: 4
Total Time: 30 minutes + marinating

I absolutely love skirt steak; the long, fatty, fibrous strip of meat is tender and flavorful with nothing more than cooking over a fire. Skirt steak is commonly found in Mexican or Latin grocery stores. Don't be shy—give it a try!

Ingredients

2 pounds skirt steak
2 tbsp All Purpose Grilling Rub (page 330)

Citrus Marinade Ingredients

4 oranges
2 limes
1 cup sliced onions
1/2 cup cilantro
1 jalapeño pepper, sliced
2 serrano peppers, sliced
1 12 oz. beer
2 tbsp minced garlic

Citrus Marinade Instructions

1. Slice the oranges and limes in half and squeeze juice into a bowl.
2. Add onion, cilantro, jalapeños, serranos, beer, and garlic to the same bowl and mix well.
3. Pour the marinade into a 1-gallon or bigger storage bag and add the skirt steak. Squeeze out all the air and seal the bag tightly.
4. Marinate the steak overnight.

Carne Asada Instructions

1. Prepare the grill for direct grilling.
2. Add red oak chunks to the charcoal. Mesquite wood is also a great substitute.
3. Temps between 500 and 600 degrees F are ideal.
4. Remove skirt steak from storage bag and pat it dry with paper towels.
5. Apply the dry rub to both sides.
6. Place skirt steak directly over the hot coals.
7. Cook 5 minutes per side. Watch it so it does not burn.
8. Grill until meat is well done. Remove steak from the grill and let it rest for a couple of minutes.

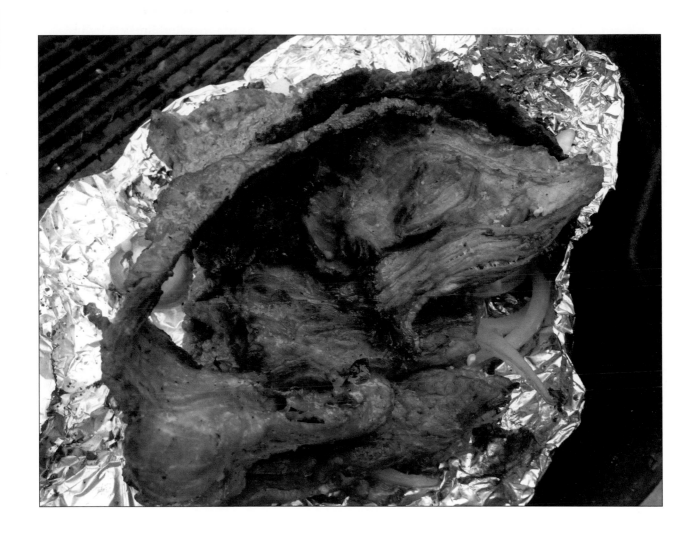

COCHINITA PIBIL

Serves: 6
Total Time: 3 hours + marinating

Ingredients

5 pounds pork butt, cut into 2-inch cubes

1 package of anchiote paste (100grams)

2 tsp ground cumin seeds

1 tbsp black pepper

1/2 tsp ground cloves

1/2 tsp ground allspice

2 jalapeño peppers, minced (keep some seeds)

1/2 cup orange juice

1/2 cup white vinegar

8 garlic cloves

2 tbsp salt

Juice of 5 lemons

1 shot of tequila

Banana leaves (optional)

Marinade Instructions

1. Combine the anchiote paste, cumin, pepper, cloves, and allspice in a blender.

2. Add the chopped jalapeño peppers, along with the orange juice, vinegar, garlic, and salt.

3. Blend the dry spices with the liquids until smooth.

4. Add the lemon juice and the tequila. Blend again until well mixed.

5. Place the cubed pork butt in a large 2-gallon resealable storage bag and add the marinade. Marinate for a few hours or overnight in the refrigerator.

After Marinating Instructions

1. Line a foil pan with banana leaves. Pour pork butt along with marinade into the center of the pan. Note: Banana leaves are not necessary. The same effect can be achieved with aluminum foil. However, it looks really cool with the banana leaves.

2. Place the foil pan on the grill. Keep the banana leaves or foil partially opened to allow smoke to penetrate the meat.

3. Smoke at around 350 degrees F for 1 hour.

4. Cover the pork with banana leaves and seal the pan with foil.

5. Continue to cook for 1 to 2 hours, until tender at approximately 200 degrees F internal temperature.

6. When the pork is done, remove from the grill and rest for 1 hour or until the pork is cool enough to handle.

7. Serve immediately.

SMOKED PORK TAMALES

Serves: 40–50
Total Time: 10 hours, 10 minutes

If there was a cooking marathon, tamales would win. Around Christmas my family takes a day or two off plus the weekend to start making tamales. They are not hard to make, but the volume of tamales made out of a pork butt is challenging. Either know a lot of people who will want tamales (which is usually the case) or make sure you have a lot of freezer space. My smoked pork tamales have really been a showstopper on my blog.

Ingredients

5 1/2-pound bone-in pork butt
Canola oil
1 cup beer
1 bag of guajillo chiles (yields 14 chiles per bag)
2 1/2 cups water
80 dried corn husks (soaked in water overnight)
5 pounds pre-made masa

Rub Ingredients

2 tbsp Hungarian paprika
1 tsp ground green jalapeño pepper
1 tsp ground white pepper
1 tbsp dark roasted chili powder
1/2 tsp Worcestershire powder
1 tbsp oregano
1 tbsp ground cumin
1/2 tsp ground cinnamon
1 tsp granulated garlic
1 tsp Kosher salt

Pork Instructions

1. Mix all rub ingredients in a bowl, reserving 1/2 cup for the chile sauce.
2. Rinse pork in water and pat dry.
3. Drizzle oil all over pork butt.
4. Cover all sides of pork butt with rub.
5. Set up smoker to 375 to 400 degrees F.
6. Place meat on the smoker. Add apple wood to the charcoal for flavor.
7. After 2 hours, wrap pork in aluminum foil, pour beer inside, and place the meat back on the smoker.
8. Let pork steam in aluminum foil for 2 hours or until bone pulls out cleanly.
9. Rest pork butt for 1 hour or until it is cool enough to handle.
10. Pull the pork into finely shredded pieces.

Chile Sauce Instructions

1. Roast the chiles on the grill. Do not burn them.
2. Soak the chiles for 2 hours in a large container.
3. Deseed all the chiles and place them in a blender, reserving soaking water.
4. Add reserved rub to the blender.

5. Take 2 cups from the chile-soaking water to add to the blender, using a strainer to keep debris out.

6. Blend until smooth.

Tamales Instructions

1. Pour masa into a large mixing bowl.

2. Add 2 cups of chile sauce to the masa and mix well.

3. Pour just enough chile sauce onto the pork to coat it well. Mix well. (Save any extra chile sauce for making chili con carne.)

4. Take a corn husk and spread the masa on it with a spoon. Spread the masa all the way to the wide edge of the corn husk while leaving a finger length with no masa at the narrow end.

The masa should be about the thickness of a tortilla.

5. Add a spoonful of pork to the center of each corn husk.

6. Overlap one side of the corn husk to the other and tuck the narrow end to form a pocket.

7. Repeat the process until all of the ingredients are gone.

8. Prepare the tamalera (tamale steam pot), by adding water to the bottom of the pot and bringing it to a boil.

9. Place all the tamales in the tamalera and steam for 1 hour or until the masa is no longer doughy.

10. Let tamales cool down before handling.

CHICKEN MOLE

Serves: 4
Total Time: 2 hours

My mom made chicken mole (pronounced MO-lay) in a slow cooker and I loved it. However, I wanted to 'Que it up a little. The smoky scent and the charred skin enhance the flavor. This is one recipe I cook often on a Sunday.

Ingredients

4 chicken leg quarters
2 tbsp MLG Poultry Rub
3 cups chicken broth
2 tbsp canola oil
1 jar Doña Maria Mole
1 cup peanut butter, creamy

MLG Poultry Rub Ingredients

1 tbsp garlic salt
1 tbsp onion powder
1/2 tbsp chili powder
1/2 tbsp paprika
1/4 tbsp black pepper

MLG Poultry Rub Instructions

1. Make the rub by combining all the rub ingredients in a bowl and mix well.

Instructions

1. Pour the chicken broth into a saucepan and bring it to a boil.
2. Empty the jar of mole paste and peanut butter into an 11.75 x 9.5 x 2.5-inch disposable foil pan.
3. Pour the hot broth over the mole and peanut butter to dissolve it.
4. Help the mole and peanut butter dissolve by working it with a fork or spoon. Don't worry if not all of it dissolves; it will during the cooking process.
5. Set up the grill for indirect heat.
6. Coat the chicken with the oil and season with the rub.
7. Add a chunk or two of hard wood (I used red oak) to the charcoal and directly grill the chicken over the coals for a few minutes until you get some grill marks. *The chicken will not be thoroughly cooked on the inside.*
8. Place the foil pan filled with the mole sauce on the cool side, opposite the charcoal coals.
9. Submerge the chicken in the mole sauce.
10. Close the lid and manage the cooking chamber temperature to 350 to 400 degrees F.
11. Rotate and flip the chicken every 15 minutes.

12. Chicken is done after 1 hour or when it reaches an internal temperature of 165 degrees F.

Notes:

1. Sauce consistency is up to you. Add more chicken broth or water if the sauce gets too thick.

2. You may also use regular oak, mesquite, hickory, or any fruit woods for this recipe.

3. Optional: Serve chicken with rice, pouring the mole sauce over everything. Top the chicken with sesame seeds and make some corn tortillas while the grill is still hot.

BRISKET ENCHILADAS

Serves: 4
Total Time: 1 hour

Ingredients

1 pound smoked brisket

1/4 cup yellow onions, diced

1 Anaheim chile pepper, roasted and diced

Salt and pepper, to taste

4 flour tortillas

2 cups Red Chile Sauce (page 335)

8 oz. cheddar cheese, shredded

1 oz. green onion, chopped

2 oz. black olives, sliced

Instructions

1. In a saucepan on medium heat, add brisket, yellow onions, and diced peppers. Season the mixture with salt and pepper. Cook until the onions are soft, and set aside.

2. Warm the tortillas and fill each one with pound of meat, roll into a burrito, and place in a foil pan.

3. Set up the grill for two-zone indirect cooking at 350 degrees F.

4. Top the tortilla rolls with 1 cup Red Chile Sauce, cheese, green onions, and olives. Cover the foil pan with a sheet of aluminum foil. Cook enchiladas on the grill for 30 minutes or until the cheese is melted. Halfway through the cooking process, add the remaining cup of chile sauce over the enchiladas.

5. Remove the foil pan from the cooker and discard the foil cover. Cool for 5 minutes.

6. Serve immediately.

Note:

Sour cream and guacamole are excellent condiments for enchiladas.

SMOKED PORK TAQUITOS

Serves: 30
Total Time: 10 hours + marinating

A New Year's tradition at my house: bowl games, parades, and a bowl of guacamole the size of a space satellite dish.

Ingredients

5-pound bone-in pork butt
30 ct yellow corn tortillas
Canola oil for deep fryer

Chile Injection Ingredients

12 dried peppers (8 pasillas, 4 ancho)
1/2 medium onion
1 tbsp chopped cilantro
1 tbsp cumin
1/2 tsp oregano
1/2 cup bitter orange juice
4 cloves of garlic
1 chicken bouillon cube
Salt and pepper

Mexican Rub Ingredients

1 tsp coarse black pepper
1 tsp sea salt
1 tsp ground oregano
1 tsp minced dried onion
1 tsp minced dried garlic

Chile Injection Instructions

1. Roast the chiles on the grill. Do not burn them.
2. Soak the chiles for 2 hours in a large container.
3. Reserve 1 cup of the water the chiles were soaking in.
4. Deseed all the chiles and place them in a food processor or blender.
5. Place all remaining ingredients into the blender.
6. Add reserved water (more if needed).
7. Blend until smooth.
8. Place the pork in a deep foil pan. Then use a meat syringe to inject the shoulder with the liquid marinade, reserving 2 cups of marinade. Afterward, cover the pan with a sheet of foil and keep it in the fridge overnight.

Smoked Pork Instructions

1. Prepare the smoker for 225 degrees F.
2. Take pork shoulder out of the fridge and uncover. Drain any liquid out of the pan.
3. Mix all Mexican Rub ingredients together and spread it evenly all over the shoulder. Make sure to get those folds and creases in between.
4. Place the pork butt on the smoker. I used pecan wood for smoke and I place a meat thermometer in the thickest part of the shoulder.
5. Cook pork until it reaches 195 degrees F internal temperature.

6. Remove pork from the smoker and let it rest at room temperature for 1 hour or until it's cool enough to shred.

Warming Tortillas

1. Since the smoker won't be hot enough to quickly warm the tortillas, I suggest using a top oven burner to warm the round yellow floppy discs.

2. Preheat the burner to medium. Place a tortilla on the burner and leave it for 10 seconds. Flip the tortilla to cook the other side for another 10 seconds. Don't burn the tortilla!

3. Place the cooked tortilla in a tortilla warmer or completely wrap in aluminum foil so they remain soft as you cook all thirty tortillas.

Frying Taquitos Instructions

1. Place a spoonful of shredded pork to one side of a warm tortilla and roll it up tightly. Repeat until all pork and tortillas are used. Stick a couple of toothpicks in each taquito to hold together.

2. Prepare a deep fryer with canola oil at medium to medium-high heat or 375 degrees F.

3. In the deep fryer, cook about 4 taquitos at a time for 4 minutes.

4. Remove the taquitos onto a plate covered with paper towels to soak up the oil, discarding toothpicks when cooled.

5. Repeat this process until done.

6. Serve taquitos with guacamole.

PORK BELLY CARNITAS WITH SALSA VERDE

Serves: 2
Total Time: 2 1/2 hours

Ingredients

1 pound pork belly, cut into 1-inch cubes
1/4 pound tomatillos
2 Anaheim peppers
2 poblano peppers
1 yellow squash
1 garlic bulb, peeled
1/2 yellow onion
2 tbsp cumin, ground
2 tbsp Mexican oregano, dried
2 chicken bouillon cubes
2 cups water
2 cups Mexican beer
2 bay leaves
Salt and pepper

Instructions

1. Setup cooker for indirect heat at 250 degrees F.

2. In a large skillet, brown the top and bottom of the pork belly cubes until they develop a crust.

3. Give tomatillos, peppers, squash, garlic, and onion a rough chop and put them in a food processor.

4. Add cumin, oregano, bouillon cubes, and water to the food processor and puree all ingredients to make salsa verde.

5. Place the pork belly cubes in a foil pan and pour the salsa verde over the top. Add beer and bay leaves, and season with salt and pepper to taste.

6. Cover foil pan with aluminum foil and place on the grill. Cook for 2 hours.

7. Carnitas are done when the cubes are tender. Serve immediately with some corn tortillas.

Tips

1. To infuse with smoke, place the pork belly cubes directly on the grill (before adding to the foil pan) and cook for 10 minutes.

2. Roast tomatillos, peppers, squash, garlic, and onion on the grill for a smoky salsa verde.

CHORIZO AND POTATOES

Serves: 3
Total Time: 1 hour

Ingredients

2 cups Yukon Gold potatoes, diced

2 cups sweet potatoes, diced

2 tbsp vegetable oil

Kosher salt

Black pepper

1 pound pork chorizo sausage

1 small yellow onion, diced

1 cup cheddar cheese, shredded

Cilantro

3 flour tortillas (optional)

Instructions

1. Set up the cooker for direct heat cooking at 350 degrees F.

2. Combine potatoes and oil in a cast-iron skillet over direct heat on the grill. Season with salt and pepper and close the lid. Cook for 30 minutes until tender.

3. In a foil pan, crumble up the sausage and add the onion and potatoes. Place over direct heat on the grill and close the lid. Cook until the sausage is done and the onion is tender, about 15 minutes.

4. In the last 5 minutes of cooking, add the cheese and let it melt.

5. Remove from the grill and garnish with cilantro.

6. Wrap in tortillas to serve as a burrito if desired, or eat as is.

STEAK AND EGG BREAKFAST WRAP

Serves: 4
Total Time: 1 hour

Ingredients

6 tbsp canola oil
1 medium Yukon Gold potato
Sea salt and pepper
1 cup Carne Asada, cooked (page 196)
5 large eggs
4 flour tortillas
1/2 cup shredded cheddar cheese (optional)
Pico de gallo (optional)
Hot sauce (optional)

Instructions

1. Set a cast-iron skillet on a gas grill and pour in the oil.
2. Close the lid and wait for it to heat up to 400 degrees F.
3. While the grill is preheating, dice up the potato into 1/4-inch cubes.
4. Place the diced potatoes in the skillet once it reaches temperature.
5. Season potatoes with salt and pepper and then stir to coat with oil.
6. Close the lid and cook for 15 minutes.
7. Chop the Carne Asada into little pieces. Note: Bulk sausage or chopped bacon is a great substitute if you do not have skirt steak.
8. After 15 minutes, the potatoes should be turning brown and looking tender.
9. Pour the meat into the skillet, stir, and continue to cook for about 10 minutes.
10. Add the eggs and scramble everything in the skillet.
11. While the skillet is cooking the meat, potato, and eggs, turn your other grill burners on so you can heat up the tortillas. These only take about 30 seconds of continuous flipping for each tortilla.
12. Assemble burritos by filling warm tortillas with the potato mixture. Sprinkle the cheese and spoon some pico de gallo over the filling, if using. Add hot sauce to the burrito for some extra heat.
13. Serve warm.

ACHIOTE WHITE WINE CHICKEN

Serves: 4

Total Time: 3 hours + marinating

Ingredients

1 whole chicken

Vegetable oil

2 tbsp MLG Poultry Rub (page 330)

Marinade Ingredients

2 oz. annatto seeds

1 tsp epazote, dried

1 bottle chardonnay

1 tbsp Mexican oregano, dried

1 bulb garlic, chopped

2 shallots, chopped

1 jalapeño, chopped

1/4 cup vegetable oil

Marinade Instructions

1. Use a spice grinder to grind up annatto seeds and epazote.

2. Combine all marinade ingredients in a 2-gallon storage bag and mix well.

Cooking Instructions

1. Spatchcock the chicken (see page 17).

2. Place chicken into the storage bag and marinate overnight in the refrigerator.

3. Setup cooker for indirect heat at 250 degrees F.

4. Remove chicken from marinade and dry off with paper towel.

5. Apply vegetable oil on bone side and season with MLG Poultry Rub. Repeat on skin side.

6. Place chicken on the cool side of the grill, skin side down, and cook for 2 hours.

7. Chicken is done when the dark meat reaches 165 degrees F.

8. Cut the bird into thighs, legs, breasts, and wings.

9. Serve immediately.

SMOKED LENGUA TACOS

You may not know this: lengua is beef tongue. Now that I may have grossed you out, beef tongue is delicious. Typically, lengua is cooked in stews, but tacos are very popular because they're portable. There's no other way to put this—you either are intrigued by this recipe or you have already moved on.

Serves: 12
Total Time: 8 hours

Ingredients

1 beef tongue
1 tbsp All Purpose Grilling Rub
2 cups beef broth
1 cup Mexican beer
12 corn tortillas
1 cup white onion, diced
1/4 cup cilantro, chopped
1 tbsp canola oil

Instructions

1. Apply rub on exposed meat (not the skin).
2. Set up the smoker at 250 degrees F. Add cherry wood chunks for smoke.
3. Smoke the beef for 1 hour.
4. Fill a foil pan with broth and beer.
5. Place beef in pan and cover with foil.
6. Cook until meat reaches 200 degrees F internal temperature (about 6 hours) and then let cool.
7. Remove beef from the foil pan, peel off skin, and discard.
8. Dice the beef into small chunks of meat.
9. Assemble tacos by warming up the tortillas and filling each one with beef, onion, and cilantro.
10. Serve immediately.

CHORIZO STUFFED CHICKEN BREAST

Serves: 2

Total Time: 1 hour + brining time

Ingredients

2 chicken breasts, bone in and skin on

2 tbsp green peppers, diced

2 tbsp white onion, finely chopped

1/4 pound beef chorizo

1/2 cup Monterey Jack cheese, shredded

MLG Pollo Brine

4 cups water

1/2 cup Kosher salt

1/2 cup white sugar

4 sprigs thyme

1 lemon peel

1 shallot, chopped

1 tbsp garlic, minced

MLG Pollo Rub

1 tsp garlic salt

1 tsp chili powder

1/2 tsp white pepper

1/4 tsp thyme, ground

1/4 tsp marjoram, ground

Instructions

1. Prepare brine: add water to saucepan and bring to a boil. Turn down to a simmer, add salt and sugar, and stir until dissolved. Let brine cool and pour into a 1-gallon storage bag. Add remaining brine ingredients and submerge chicken in the brine. Place in the refrigerator overnight.

2. Setup cooker for indirect heat at 500+ degrees F with the lid off the cooker.

3. Cook peppers in cast iron skillet over direct heat until they start to soften. Remove from skillet and let cool.

4. Mix peppers, onions, chorizo and cheese together in a bowl. Set aside. In another bowl, combine rub ingredients.

5. Wipe brine off the chicken with paper towels and using a sharp knife, cut a pocket into each chicken breast.

6. Spoon the chorizo mixture into the chicken and season both sides with rub.

7. Over direct heat, cook chicken on cast iron skillet for 5 minutes on each side.

8. Move the skillet to the cool side of the cooker, close the cook chamber by placing the lid on. Let the cooker come down to 350 degrees F and cook for 40 minutes or until chicken reaches 155 degrees F.

9. Remove chicken from cooker and serve.

ACHIOTE STEAK TACOS

Serves: 4

Total Time: 30 minutes + marinating

Ingredients

2 pounds skirt steak

4 flour tortillas

1 cup Sautéed onions and peppers or 1/2 cup
    onions and 1/2 cup green onions, sautéed.

Achiote Marinade Ingredients

1/2 package of achiote paste (50 grams)

1 tsp ground cumin

1/2 tbsp black pepper

1/4 tsp ground cloves

1/4 tsp ground allspice

1 jalapeño peppers, rough chop (optional)

2 Fresno peppers, rough chop (optional)

1/4 cup bitter orange juice

1/4 cup red wine vinegar

4 garlic cloves

1 tbsp sea salt

Juice of 5 small lemons

1 shot tequila

Achiote Marinade Instructions

1. Combine the achiote paste, cumin, pepper, cloves, and allspice in a food processor or blender. Add the chopped jalapeño and Fresno peppers with the orange juice, vinegar, garlic and salt. Blend the dry spices with the liquid until smooth.

2. Add the juice of lemons and the tequila. Blend again until well mixed.

Achiote Steak Tacos Instructions

1. Place the skirt steak in a large 2-gallon storage bag and add the marinade. Marinate for a few hours or overnight in the refrigerator.

2. Setup the grill for direct cooking. Get a hot grill at 600+ degrees F. I used peach wood for smoky flavor, but any fruit wood is ideal.

3. Cook the steak until a crust starts to form on the underside. Flip and repeat.

4. When both sides are seared, remove from the grill and let them rest on a plate for 5 minutes.

5. Slice the steak against the grain into strips.

6. Warm up some flour tortillas and sauté onions and peppers for a great taco.

7. Layer steak, onions, and peppers on warmed tortillas and serve immediately.

CARNE ASADA FRIES

Serves: 6
Total Time: 1 hour

Ingredients

1 pound skirt steak
2 tbsp All Purpose Grilling Rub (page 330)
1 pound waffle fries, frozen
1 cup shredded cheddar cheese
1/4 cup crema
1/2 cup Pico de Gallo (see below)
1/2 cup diced avocado
1/2 cup grated cotija cheese

Pico de Gallo

2 Roma tomatoes, diced
1 jalapeño, deseeded, deveined, and diced
1/2 cup diced white onion
1 tbsp chopped cilantro
2 tbsp lime juice
1/2 tsp Kosher salt

Instructions

1.   Prepare the Pico de Gallo: mix all ingredients together and refrigerate until ready to use. Set up the cooker for direct heat grilling at 400+ degrees F.

2.   Apply the rub on the skirt steak and let it sit at room temperature for a few minutes to let the meat absorb the seasonings.

3.   Meanwhile, prepare the waffle fries according to the package instructions.

4.   Grill the steaks over high heat until the meat starts to char a little or until medium, 140 degrees F internal temperature. Remove from the grill and slice the steak against the grain and then wrap the steak in aluminum foil and set aside.

5.   In a foil pan, add the waffle fries and top with the steak. Sprinkle the cheddar cheese over the top and melt on the grill or in the oven.

6.   Pile on the toppings starting with the crema first, followed by Pico de Gallo, avocado, and cotija.

7.   Serve immediately.

RIB-EYE FAJITA TORTA

Serves: 2
Total Time: 40 minutes

Tortas are sandwiches, typically found in taquerias (taco shops). This sandwich is so good, it should be on a menu—I'd buy it! Delicioso!

Ingredients

1/2 medium white onion, sliced
1/2 green pepper, sliced and deseeded
2 tbsp olive oil
1 avocado
1/2 tsp Kosher salt
1/2 tsp lime juice
2 tbsp mayonnaise
1 tbsp Sriracha Chili Sauce
1 pound rib-eye steak, sliced wafer thin
2 hot dogs, cut in half lengthwise
1 slice Monterey Jack cheese
1 Kaiser roll
1 fried egg

Instructions

1. Setup grill for indirect heat at 400 degrees F.

2. In a foil pocket, combine the onions, peppers, and 1 tbsp olive oil. Seal foil tight and place it directly over the fire. Close the cooking chamber and cook for 20 minutes.

3. Peel the skin and remove the pit from the avocado. Place avocado in a bowl and mash with a fork or potato masher. Add the salt and lime juice. Mix well, and refrigerate until ready to use.

4. Combine mayonnaise and chili sauce together in a small bowl. Refrigerate until ready to use.

5. After the peppers and onions have cooked for 20 minutes, coat sliced steak and hot dogs with the rest of the olive oil and cook directly over the fire. These cook quickly, so as soon as they are done, remove from the grill and set aside on a plate. Place a slice of cheese over the pile of steak and cover with foil for a minute.

6. Slice the roll into a bun and spread the mayonnaise mix inside. Pile on the steak and cheese, peppers and onions, avocado, hot dogs, and fried egg.

7. Serve immediately.

ALBONDIGAS WITH CHIPOTLE SAUCE

Serves: 4
Total Time: 1 hour

Ingredients

1 pound ground chuck
1/2 pound ground pork
1/4 cup milk
1 egg
1/2 cup cooked rice
1/2 tsp ground cumin
1/2 cup bread crumbs
1 tsp oregano
Salt and pepper
1 recipe Chipotle Sauce (page 336)
1/2 medium onion, sliced
Cilantro, for garnish
Cooked rice, for serving (optional)

Instructions

1. Combine ground chuck, ground pork, milk, egg, rice, cumin, bread crumbs, and oregano together in a large bowl. Add salt and pepper to taste, and mix well.

2. Form approximately 8 large meatballs, about 2 inches in diameter.

3. Set up the cooker for indirect heat at 350 degrees F.

4. Place the meatballs on the cool side of the grill where there is no heat source.

5. Pour Chipotle Sauce into a foil pan and place on the hot side of the grill.

6. Cook for 10 minutes with the lid on and vents wide open.

7. Next, place all the meatballs and the sliced onion into the foil pan.

8. Move the foil pan to the cool side of the grill.

9. Check the fire, and add more charcoal if needed.

10. Close the lid with the vents wide open.

11. Cook for 30 to 45 minutes, depending on the size of your meatballs.

12. Meatballs are done when the internal temperature reaches 160 degrees.

13. Garnish with cilantro and serve as is or with rice.

SINCRONIZADAS (HAM AND CHEESE MELT)

Serves: 2
Total Time: 15 minutes

Ingredients

1 tortilla, extra large (12 inches)
1/2 cup refried pinto beans, from a can
4 oz. Oaxaca cheese, sliced
1/4 pound smoked ham
2 tbsp canola oil

Garnish
Crema
Roasted Salsa (page 290)
Cilantro

Instructions

1. Setup cooker for indirect heat with the lid off to cook over the coals at 500+ degrees F.

2. On a flat, clean surface, lay out tortilla and cover half of it with a thin layer of beans.

3. Add cheese and ham over the beans.

4. Fold tortilla in half and brush on a coat of oil.

5. Cook directly over the fire until tortilla develops grill marks. Flip and repeat.

6. Move tortilla melt to the cool side of the grill, close the cooking chamber, and cook for 5 minutes.

7. Remove from grill and cut the melt into 4 wedges using a pizza cutter.

8. Garnish with crema, salsa, and cilantro.

9. Serve immediately.

SMOKY CHARRO BEANS

Serves: 6
Total Time: 3 hours, 10 minutes

Ingredients

3 cups dried pinto beans

4 Roma tomatoes

1/2 medium sweet onion, diced

1/2 green pepper, diced

1/4 cup chopped cilantro

1 jalapeño, veins and seeds removed, diced

2 cloves garlic, chopped

6 slices cooked bacon, chopped

1 beef bouillon cube

Cerveza

Instructions

1. On the stove on high heat, bring a large pot of water to a boil. Add beans, and turn the heat down to medium.

2. Cook beans for two hours or until they are almost soft, then drain them.

3. Place the beans, vegetables, and bacon in a foil pan.

4. Set up the grill for direct heat grilling at 375 degrees F.

5. Place foil pan on the grill.

6. Add the bouillon cube, and enough cerveza to cover the beans.

7. Mix occasionally, adding cerveza when necessary to keep beans from drying out.

8. Cook the beans 30 minutes to 1 hour or until tender and the liquid is almost gone.

9. Serve immediately.

CHAPTER 6

FAMILY COOKOUT FAVORITES

CLASSIC PULLED PORK

Serves: 6
Cook Time: 7 hours

Every pitmaster can ace this recipe in Barbecue 101. Great barbecue starts with making a killer pulled pork. Are you up to the challenge?

Ingredients
5-pound pork butt (bone-in)
1/4 cup canola oil
1/4 cup MLG BBQ Rub (see below)
1 cup apple juice
MLG Barbecue Sauce (see below)

MLG BBQ Rub Ingredients
1/2 cup turbinado sugar
3 tbsp Kosher salt,
1 tbsp garlic powder
1 tbsp onion powder
1 tbsp chili powder
1 tbsp Hungarian paprika
1 tbsp black pepper
1/2 tsp cayenne pepper

MLG BBQ Rub Instructions
1. Combine all ingredients in a bowl and mix well.

MLG Barbecue Sauce Ingredients
1/2 cup unsalted butter
3 cloves garlic, minced
1/2 small yellow onion, chopped
1/2 green pepper, chopped
1/4 cup bourbon
1/2 cup dark brown sugar
1/2 cup light corn syrup
2 cups ketchup
2 cups water
1 tbsp unsulfured blackstrap molasses
1/4 cup apple cider vinegar
2 tsp Kosher salt
1 tbsp red pepper flakes
1/2 tbsp black pepper

MLG Barbecue Sauce Instructions
1. In a saucepan on medium heat, melt the butter and add garlic, onions, and green peppers. Cook until they are soft.
2. Add the remaining ingredients and mix well.
3. Let the sauce simmer and slightly thicken for about 10 minutes.
4. Remove from the heat and let it cool.
5. Pour the sauce into a food processor and blend until smooth.
6. Use immediately or store in a jar with a lid and refrigerate.

Cooking Instructions

1. Set up smoker at 250 degrees F.

2. Apply oil on the pork butt, then coat with rub.

3. Place the pork on the grate, add a chunk of apple wood, and smoke for 5 hours.

4. In a foil pan, add apple juice and place pork butt in the pan. Cover pan with aluminum foil and cook for 2 hours.

5. The pork is done when the meat can easily be pulled apart. If not, cook another 30 minutes. If using a meat thermometer, anything over 200 degrees F is considered done.

6. Cook uncovered in the foil pan for an additional 30 minutes.

7. Rest pork butt for 30 minutes or until cool enough to handle.

8. Pull and serve immediately. (see page xx)

SMOKED MEATLOAF

Serves: 6–8
Total Time: 2 hours, 30 minutes

Smoked meatloaf wins by a wide margin, according to my kids. They absolutely love when I make the bacon weave around this football-sized loaf. Check out the bacon weave tutorial on page 26.

Ingredients

2 pounds ground beef
1 cup milk
2 tsp chopped fresh basil
1/2 tsp sea salt
1/2 tsp ground mustard
1/4 tsp pepper
1 tbsp garlic powder
1 tbsp Worcestershire sauce
1 egg
3/4 cup crushed Saltine crackers
1/4 cup diced onion
1/2 cup diced green pepper
1/4 cup Andria's Steak Sauce
14 slices bacon
BBQ Sauce (page 332)

Instructions

1.   Mix all of the ingredients together in a bowl except for the bacon and the BBQ Sauce.

2.   Place the raw meatloaf in the refrigerator and get out the bacon.

3.   Lay down a piece of plastic wrap and make a bacon weave (see page 26) on top of it so that it will be easier to cover the loaf with the bacon.

4.   Pour the meatloaf into the center of the bacon weave. Form the "loaf" on top of the bacon.

5.   Carefully roll the bacon weave over the meatloaf. Make sure the bacon slices overlap each other and the ends are rounded off. Remove and discard the plastic wrap.

6.   Set up the smoker at 230 degrees F. Add cherry and hickory wood chunks for smoke.

7.   When the grill is up to temperature, gingerly place the loaf on the grill opposite the charcoal.

8.   Place the lid on the grill making sure the vents are open on the lid and the vents are placed directly over the meat.

9.   The meat needs to reach 165 degrees F (which is well done for ground beef). Once it reaches that internal temperature, pull it off the smoker and move it over to direct heat. Grill it to crisp up the bacon (otherwise it comes off the smoker slightly soft and chewy).

10. Slice into 1/2-inch portions and serve.

BACON WRAPPED MEATBALLS

Serves: 20–25

Total Time: 1 1/2 hours

Ingredients

1-pound bag frozen meatballs, partially thawed

1 pound bacon, thin sliced and cut in half
 crosswise

BBQ Rub (page 330)

BBQ Sauce (page 332)

Instructions

1. Set up smoker at 250 degrees F. Add apple wood chunks for smoke.

2. Use toothpicks to wrap half of a bacon strip around each meatball.

3. Dust all the bacon-wrapped meatballs with the BBQ Rub.

4. Place all the meatballs on the smoker and cook for 1 hour.

5. The meatballs are done when the bacon is cooked.

6. Put the meatballs in a foil pan and brush sauce over them.

7. Serve immediately.

BLUEBERRY MUFFIN STUFFED FATTY

Serves: 12
Total Time: 2 hours

Quick story: A few years back, I was at an event giving away free samples of barbecue. It was opening day for the St. Louis Cardinals baseball team and there was a local radio station broadcasting all the festivities. I made the blueberry muffin fatty and it was a home run (pun intended)! The radio station got wind of the samples and they loved it too. They even mentioned it over the radio to draw the fans in. Some time went by and a man came up to me for a sample. He said he had heard about the fatty on the radio, and he had to stop by and try it. I had to break it to him that we were all out, and he walked away dejected. I hope that guy buys this book—now is his chance to try it.

Ingredients

1 (7oz.) box Jiffy blueberry muffin mix
1 (16 oz.) roll Jimmy Dean regular pork sausage
Maple syrup
BBQ Rub (page 330)

Instructions

1. Bake muffin mix according to directions on the box. Let muffins cool down.

2. Prepare the fatty: flatten the sausage to 1/4-inch thickness in a rectangular shape on a sheet of plastic wrap.

3. Add 2 cups of cooked muffin mix into the center of the flattened sausage.

4. Drizzle 1/3 cup maple syrup over the muffin.

5. Roll the sausage into a tube around the muffin mixture. Make sure to seal all the cracks and crevices, or the filling will tend to seep out. Apply the BBQ Rub all around the sausage.

6. Set up the cooker for indirect heat at 300 degrees F. Add peach wood chunks for smoke.

7. Smoke the fatty for 1 1/2 hours or until the internal temperature reads 165 degrees F.

8. Slice into 1/2-inch discs and serve.

PICKLED EGG POTATO SALAD

Terry Aguirre

Serves: 8–10
Total Time: 1 1/2 hours

Finally! My mom's secret recipe exposed!

Ingredients

10–12 medium russet potatoes
1 cup pickle juice
5 eggs
3 stalks celery
4 stalks green onion
1 small can of black olives, sliced
4 tbsp mayonnaise
2 tbsp mustard
Salt and pepper to taste

Instructions

1.   Boil potatoes with skin, till soft.
2.   Peel and dice potatoes.
3.   Once potatoes are cool, add pickle juice to potatoes in large bowl.
4.   Hard boil the eggs.
5.   While eggs are cooling, chop celery and green onion. When eggs are cool, peel and chop them.
6.   Add eggs, celery, green onion, and olives to cooled potatoes and fold together in large bowl.
7.   Mix mayonnaise and mustard together, then fold into potato mixture.
8.   Add salt and pepper to taste.
9.   Serve cold and enjoy.

TOMATO BASIL SALAD

Sharon Hohman

Serves: 4
Total Time: 45 minutes

Ingredients

1/2 lb cherry tomatoes
1/3 cup basil, cut in small pieces
2 tbsp of a good balsamic vinegar
3 tbsp extra virgin olive oil
1 tsp Italian seasoning
2 or 3 cloves garlic, minced
Salt and pepper to taste
1/4 cup Parmesan, mozzarella, orfeta cheese
Homemade Croutons (below)

Instructions

1. Combine tomatoes and basil in a bowl.

2. In a jar with a lid, combine balsamic vinegar, extra virgin olive oil, Italian seasoning, minced garlic, salt, and pepper.

3. Shake jar vigorously and pour mixture onto tomato and basil. Add cheese and Homemade Croutons. Toss.

Note: For full flavor of Parmesan do not shred, but cut or shave into pieces.

HOMEMADE CROUTONS

Ingredients
1 6-inch French bread cut into 1-inch cubes
1/4 cup Extra virgin olive oil
1 tbsp garlic salt
1 tbsp Italian seasoning

Instructions
1. Preheat grill to 350 degrees F.
2. Lay bread cubes in a single layer on a cookie sheet.
3. Pour extra virgin olive oil over bread and mix to coat.
4. Sprinkle garlic salt and Italian seasoning over bread.
5. Grill at 350 degrees F for approximately 10 to 15 minutes or until golden brown.
6. Cool before using.

GRILLED SNAP PEAS AND MUSHROOMS

Serves: 4
Total Time: 20 minutes

Ingredients

8 oz. sugar snap peas

8 oz. cremini mushrooms, sliced

3 tbsp olive oil

1 tsp garlic salt

1 tsp black pepper

Instructions

1.   Set up the cooker for direct heat grilling on high heat at 500+ degrees F.

2.   In a 1-gallon storage bag, combine all the ingredients and mix together.

3.   Place a grill basket directly over the heat source and dump the ingredients into the basket.

4.   Cook for about 10 minutes without the lid on the cooker, stirring as needed so the vegetables do not burn. When the mushrooms are soft and the veggies are charred a little, they are done.

5.   Pour the veggies into a bowl and serve immediately.

PICNIC MOSTACIOLLI

Serves: 6
Total Time: 45 minutes

Who's bringing the mostaciolli? When we invite family over for a barbecue, mostaciolli is always on the menu. I can't help but expect pasta with my barbecue now. Is that weird?

Ingredients

2 tbsp olive oil

2 tbsp unsalted butter

1/2 medium onion, diced

1 roasted garlic bulb

128 oz. can San Marzano tomatoes

Salt and pepper

4 tbsp sugar

1/2 pound mostaciolli, cooked

1/4 cup Parmesan cheese

Basil leaves

Instructions

1. Add olive oil, butter, and onion to a saucepan over medium heat.

2. When onion is soft, add garlic and stir.

3. Add tomatoes, using a wooden spoon to crush tomatoes in pan.

4. Cook for 30 minutes and then add salt, pepper and sugar. Taste and adjust if needed.

5. Transfer mixture to a food processor to blend sauce. Blend until smooth.

6. Pour mostaciolli and sauce into a bowl and mix well.

7. Top with cheese and garnish with basil.

8. Serve immediately.

SOUTHWEST SUMMER CORN SALAD

Jamie Aguirre

Serves: 6
Total Time: 40 minutes

Ingredients

1 red or orange sweet pepper

1 tbsp olive oil

10 oz. frozen corn

1 can black beans

1 medium red ripe tomato, chopped

1 small to medium raw red onion, diced

2 avocados, peeled and cubed

Juice of 1 lime

1/4 cup raw cilantro

1/2 tsp cumin

Salt to taste

Pepper to taste

Roasted Pepper Instructions

1. Fill kettle grill with enough charcoal to fill bottom.

2. Allow coals to get hot.

3. Place pepper directly on the grill and wait for underside to blacken.

4. Turn pepper periodically so that it blackens on all sides (you want it to look burnt).

5. Remove pepper from grill and place in a sealable plastic bag.

6. Allow pepper to steam inside the sealed bag (about 30 minutes).

7. Remove from bag, peel skin off pepper, remove the seeds, and dice the pepper.

Salad Instructions

1. Heat olive oil in cast-iron skillet on grill.

2. Add frozen corn to the pan.

3. Allow corn to warm and darken slightly (not burning or charring).

4. Place roasted corn in a bowl.

5. Drain and rinse beans and add to bowl.

6. Add chunky tomato, diced onion, diced roasted pepper, and cubes of avocado.

7. Season with lime juice, cilantro, cumin, salt, and pepper to taste.

8. Mix well and serve.

Note:

This recipe can be prepared 1 day in advance and chilled in the fridge. Add all ingredients except for the avocado. Add the avocado right before serving.

CREAMY FRUITINI SALAD

Serves: 8

Total Time: 10 minutes + 1 hour
refrigerator time

Ingredients

6 oz. strawberry yogurt

1 box cheesecake pudding mix (4-serving size),
    prepared as directed

12 oz. whipped cream

1 pound strawberries

1 cup mini marshmallows

3 bananas, sliced

Instructions

1. Mix yogurt and pudding.
2. Fold in whipped cream.
3. Add strawberries and marshmallows.
4. Chill in the refrigerator for 1 hour.
5. Add bananas and serve.

CHAPTER 7

SMALL PLATES & SIDE DISHES

JALAPEÑO POPPERS

Canadian Bakin' (Al Bowman)
Competition BBQ Team

Serves: 30
Total Time: 1 1/2 hours

Ingredients

30 jalapeños, halved lengthwise, seeds and
    membranes removed
2 packages apple- or hickory-smoked bacon, thin
    cut if available

Filling Ingredients

2 8 oz. packages cream cheese
1 tbsp brown sugar
1/2 cup shredded sharp cheddar cheese
1/4 cup your favorite barbecue sauce such
    as Nellie's Hot BBQ Sauce, plus extra for
    dusting
1 tbsp your favorite hot barbecue rub such as
    Code 3 Backdraft Rub, plus extra for basting

Instructions

1.   Combine all filling ingredients in a bowl and mix well.

2.   Fill each pepper half with filling, taking care not to over-fill.

3.   Slice strips of bacon in half crosswise. Wrap each filled pepper with a piece of bacon.

4.   Sprinkle each assembled pepper lightly with more barbecue rub.

5.   Prepare the smoker at 300 degrees F with Mojobricks cherry wood for smoke. Smoke peppers until bacon crisps, about 1 hour.

6.   During the last 10 minutes, baste peppers with more barbecue sauce.

7.   Poppers are done with the bacon is thoroughly cooked.

8.   Rest for 10 minutes and serve.

CLASSIC GRILLED CORN

Serves: 4
Total Time: 15 mintues

I've seen some crazy techniques out there regarding how to cook corn. It's one of those things that stumps folks. I keep it simple and my family prefers that I cook it this way all the time.

Ingredients

4 ears yellow corn, in the husk

Instructions

1. Set up the cooker for direct heat grilling at high heat.

2. Pull back the husk and tie it with butcher twine to make a handle, or tear off the husk and discard. Remove the corn silk and discard.

3. Place the corn directly over the heat and cook until the color becomes brighter or when the corn starts to develop charring. The corn has been cooking too long on one side if it begins to pop.

4. Flip the corn over and cook the other side.

5. Remove from the grill and serve immediately.

COLESLAW

Serves: 4
Total Time: 30 minutes

Ingredients

1/2 head cabbage, shredded
1/4 cup apple cider vinegar
1/3 cup mayonnaise
2 cloves garlic, minced
1/8 cup white sugar
2 cooked bacon strips, chopped
Salt and pepper

Instructions

1. In a bowl, whisk together apple cider vinegar, mayonnaise, garlic, and sugar.

2. Pour dressing over cabbage, add bacon, and mix well.

3. Store in the fridge until ready to use.

GARLIC FINGERLINGS

Serves: 4
Total Time: 25 minutes

Ingredients

1 1/2 pounds fingerling potatoes
1/2 cup flour
2 tbsp Italian seasoning
2 cubes vegetable bouillon
1 tsp red pepper flakes
1 tsp Kosher salt
Canola oil
1/2 cup garlic, minced
1/4 cup olive oil
2 tbsp Italian parsley
1/4 cup Asiago cheese
Salt and pepper

Instructions

1. Cut potatoes in half.

2. Fill a large pot with water, place over high heat, and bring to a boil. Add potatoes.

3. Boil potatoes for 6 to 8 minutes. Meanwhile, combine the flour, Italian seasoning, boullion, red pepper flakes and salt together in medium sized mixing bowl.

4. Drain and dry potatoes thoroughly with cloth towels. Place all the potatoes in the flour mix bowl, then give the potatoes a toss to evenly coat.

5. Prepare a deep fryer with canola oil at 375 degrees F. Deep fry fingerlings for 5 minutes.

6. Place on paper towel.

7. Set up cooker for direct grilling at high heat.

8. Roast potatoes until lightly charred.

9. Combine roasted potatoes, garlic, oil, parsley, cheese, salt, and pepper, and toss in a bowl.

10. Serve immediately.

SMOKED ACORN SQUASH

Serves: 4

Total Time: 1 hour

Ingredients

1 acorn squash

1/4 cup unsalted butter

1/2 cup hot pepper jelly

Instructions

1. Set up the cooker for indirect cooking at 300 degree F.

2. Cut the squash in half from stem to point. You need some muscles to do this. Remove and discard the seeds and pulp inside the acorn squash.

3. Pierce the skin a number of times with a knife and cook the squash in the microwave for 3 minutes to soften the squash a little.

4. Place the squash skin side down on the cool side of the grill and cook with indirect heat for 30 minutes.

5. In a saucepan, melt the butter and add the jelly. Stir to mix and keep warm.

6. Baste the squash with the butter/jelly mixture and wrap the squash in aluminum foil. Cook for 15 minutes. This will expedite the cooking process.

7. Unwrap the squash and baste again.

8. Remove from the grill when tender.

GRILLED MEXICAN STREET CORN

Chef Todd Kussman

Serves: 4–6
Total Time: 30 minutes

Ingredients

4–6 ears corn, shucked clean

1/2 cup mayonnaise

4–6 green onions, sliced thin

6 oz. queso cotija or queso fresco

1/2 tsp cumin

1/2 tsp garlic salt

Cayenne pepper, to taste

Juice of 1 lime

Instructions

1.   Grill corn over direct heat, turning often until evenly and slightly charred.

2.   Once grilled, cut the corn off cobs lengthwise and place kernels into medium bowl.

3.   Combine remaining ingredients in separate bowl and then fold into corn until mixed well.

GRILLED PEACH CAPRESE SALAD

Serves: 5–8
Total Time: 15 minutes

Ingredients

4 semi-firm peaches, pits removed
1 ball of mozzarella cheese
1/2 cup honey
1/4 tsp ancho chile powder
Nonstick spray
2 tbsp balsamic vinegar
2 tbsp olive oil
1/4 black pepper
1 oz. fresh basil

Instructions

1. Prepare peaches and cheese by slicing to same thickness and size.

2. Set up the grill for direct heat grilling at high heat.

3. Mix honey and ancho chile powder in a dish.

4. Dip the flesh sides of the peaches into the honey mixture.

5. Spray the nonstick spray on both sides of the peaches, and grill them directly over the fire. Only cook long enough to achieve grill marks.

6. Grill both sides until char marks form, and remove from the grill when they're done.

7. Arrange peaches and cheese. Top with balsamic vinegar, oil, ground pepper, and basil and serve.

ASPARAGUS RAFTS

Serves: 8
Total Time: 30 minutes

Ingredients

1 pound asparagus

4 oz. coppa salami, sliced

1 tbsp canola oil

Kosher salt

Black pepper

2 tbsp Asiago cheese

Instructions

1. Wrap a slice of coppa around 1 asparagus spear. Repeat to make as many as you can with remaining ingredients.

2. Make rafts by using 3 toothpicks to line up the asparagus side by side, like a raft. Use about 4 sticks of asparagus to build the rafts. Coat the rafts with oil and season with salt and pepper.

3. Set up the cooker for indirect heat grilling at 350 degrees F.

4. Place the rafts on the cool side of the cooker and cook using indirect heat for 15 minutes.

5. Move and cook the rafts directly over the heat source until the rafts start to develop charring.

6. Remove from the grill and immediately top the rafts with cheese.

7. Serve immediately.

MEX-SEA-CAN STUFFED POBLANO

Serves: 2

Total Time: 45 minutes

Ingredients

2 poblano peppers

1/2 pound Mexican chorizo

1/3 cup vidalia onions (rough chopped)

1/2 pound raw shrimp (de-veined and tails off)

Nonstick spray

Avocado-Cilantro Sauce

1 avocado (remove skin and seed)

1 cup light sour cream

1/4 cup cilantro

Juice of 1 lime

1/2 tsp garlic, minced

Instructions

1.   Combine Avocado-Cilantro Sauce ingredients in a food processor. Blend until smooth.

2.   Place sauce in the fridge until ready to use.

3.   Setup the grill for the two-zone method.

4.   Place the peppers directly over the hot side of the grill with the lid on until they are semi-soft and a little charred.

5.   Place chorizo and onions in a skillet and let them cook on the cool side with the lid on until the onion is soft.

6.   Check the peppers and stir the chorizo every few minutes.

7.   Spray the shrimp with oil so they don't stick to the grill grates.

8.   Cook shrimp until they're pink, add them to the skillet, and mix well.

9.   When the peppers are semi-soft, make each one into a pocket and scoop out the veins and seeds.

10.   Stuff the peppers with the chorizo and shrimp mix and put them the on the cool side of the grill with the lid on.

11.   The peppers are done when they are completely soft. Be careful—use a spatula and tongs to handle them.

12.   Apply a dollop of Avocado-Cilantro Sauce and serve immediately.

BLACKSTRAP MIXED NUTS

Serves: 6
Total Time: 25 minutes

Ingredients

10 oz. mixed nuts, raw and unsalted

1 tbsp canola oil

2 tbsp blackstrap molasses

2 tbsp white sugar

1/2 tsp chile de arbol, ground

1 tbsp Kosher salt

Instructions

1. Set up the smoker at 300 degrees F.

2. In a foil pan, evenly spread out all the nuts and add the oil.

3. Pour half of the molasses, sugar, chile, and salt over them. Mix together with a spoon to coat the nuts.

4. Place foil pan on the smoker and cook for 20 minutes.

5. Remove from the cooker and let it cool. As the nuts cool, they will stick together; keep stirring the nuts to break up the clumps and until they completely cool.

6. In the middle of cooling, add the remaining ingredients to give it some texture.

7. Serve immediately when cooled.

Note:

Optionally substitute raw nuts with roasted or lightly salted nuts.

SWEET POTATO FRIES

Serves: 4
Total Time: 15 minutes

Ingredients

Canola oil
4 medium sweet potatoes
1 tbsp BBQ Rub (page 330)
2 tbsp flour
Kosher salt

Instructions

1. Heat oil in fryer to 325 degrees F.
2. Use a french fry cutter to make sweet potatoes into fries.
3. Fry for 3 minutes. Drain on brown paper bags.
4. Raise oil to 375 degrees F.
5. Mix BBQ Rub and flour together in a small bowl. Coat fries with BBQ Rub and flour mix.
6. Fry potatoes for 4 more minutes, until golden and crispy.
7. Drain on brown paper, lightly season with Kosher salt, serve immediately.

JULI'S BAKED BEANS

Juli Getzlaf

Serves: 6
Total Time: 1 hour

Ingredients

1 pound ground beef (sirloin or chuck)

1 pound good hickory-smoked bacon, cut in bite-size pieces (use ends and pieces or thick cut for best flavor and meatiness)

1 pound hickory-smoked sausage (such as Conecuh), cut in bite-size pieces

2 medium onions or 1 large Texas or yellow onion, chopped

3 large bell peppers, chopped (one each, red, yellow, and green)

4–6 cloves of fresh garlic, minced

4 1 lb 12 oz. Bush's Original Baked Beans

1/2 cup ketchup

1/4–1/2 cup brown sugar, either dark or light

Large squirt of yellow mustard

1/3 jar Grandma's Molasses

Spice Mix

1 tbsp onion powder or granules

1 tbsp garlic powder or granules

1 tbsp smoked paprika

1 tbsp Coleman's Dry Mustard

1 tbsp red pepper seasoning

Salt and pepper to taste

Instructions

1. Preheat oven or grill to 375°F.

2. Prepare Spice Mix by combining all ingredients in a small bowl. Brown ground beef, season with Spice Mix, drain, and set aside.

3. Cook bacon in frying pan. It should not be crispy. Set aside.

4. Cook sausage until brown and set aside.

5. Sauté onions and peppers. Add minced garlic for the last minute or two so it doesn't burn.

6. Once beef, bacon, sausage, and vegetables are ready, combine in a large baking pan with remaining ingredients.

7. Bake in oven for 45 minutes uncovered or on grill until heated through, about 30 minutes. You will know it is done once the sauce thickens and turns darker brown.

8. Keep wrapped in foil until ready to enjoy!

Note:

You can add some diced ham and a little hot sauce for flavor as well.

GRILLED GUACAMOLE

Serves: 6
Total Time: 30 minutes

Not that guacamole needs to be grilled, but I found that an avocado that was a little firm will soften when cooked. A brief grilling for grill marks is good enough for all the vegetables and fruit, but cooking too long is off-putting. When done right, the guacamole will have a hint of a smoky scent.

Ingredients

5 avocados
1 tomato
4 tbsp olive oil
1 lime, cut in half
2 green onions
1/4 cup fresh cilantro
1 tsp salt

Instructions

1. Prep grill for high heat (600+ degrees F).
2. Cut the avocados in half and remove the seed from each fruit.
3. Cut the tomato into 8 equal wedges.
4. Pour the olive oil and squeeze half of a lime into a small dish.
5. Brush the oil and lime onto the flesh of the avocado (no need to brush the skin).
6. Brush the oil and lime onto the tomato and the other half of the lime.
7. Place all the avocados, tomatoes, and lime on the grill, flesh side down.
8. After about 1 minute, turn the avocado and lime 90 degrees and flip the tomatoes.
9. After another minute, remove all the fruits from the grill.
10. Peel the skin off the avocados and place them in a bowl.
11. Smash them with a potato masher or fork.
12. Dice all the tomatoes and add them to the bowl.
13. Add the green onions, cilantro, juice of the grilled half of the lime, and salt.
14. Mix all the ingredients together.

GRILLED ROMAINE WITH HOT BACON DRESSING

Serves: 4
Total Time: 20 minutes

Ingredients

2 hearts of romaine lettuce
1/4 cup olive oil
Kosher salt
Black pepper

Hot Bacon Dressing Ingredients

2 tbsp bacon grease
2 tbsp honey
1 tsp grainy mustard
1/4 cup onion, chopped
1 tbsp apple cider vinegar
1/2 cup water
1/2 tbsp cornstarch and 1 tbsp cold water, stirred
   into a paste
2 strips cooked bacon, crumbled
Salt and pepper

Instructions

1. To prepare the dressing: In a saucepan, cook bacon grease, honey, mustard, onions, vinegar, and water on medium heat until it begins to boil. Add the cornstarch paste and stir as the dressing starts to thicken. Remove from the heat and set aside at room temperature. Stir in the bacon and season with salt and pepper.

2. Set up the cooker for direct heat grilling at high heat.

3. Cut the romaine in half from stem to point.

4. Coat the flat area of the lettuce with oil and season with salt and pepper.

5. Cook the lettuce over direct heat for just a few minutes, until it begins charring.

6. Remove from the grill and drizzle the dressing over the lettuce.

7. Serve immediately.

BBQ RANCH CRACKERS

Serves: 12–14
Total Time: 20 minutes

Ingredients
4 sleeves Saltine crackers
1 1/2 cup canola oil
3 tbsp red pepper flakes
1 package ranch dressing mix

Instructions
1. Set up the cooker for indirect heat grilling at 350 degrees F.

2. In a 2-gallon storage bag, combine all ingredients and mix well for several minutes. Try not to break any crackers—a light tumble in the bag does the trick.

3. Pour the crackers into a foil pan. Cover and seal with a sheet of aluminum foil.

4. Place the foil pan directly over the heat source and cook for 5 minutes.

5. Move the pan over to the cool side of the grill and cook for 10 minutes.

6. Remove the pan from the grill, remove the foil, and give the crackers a gentle toss.

7. Serve immediately.

CHAPTER 8

SEAFOOD RECIPES

MEXICAN SALMON WITH ROASTED SALSA

Serves: 4
Total Time: 1 hour

Ingredients

1 1/2 pounds wild Alaskan salmon (skin on), 6 oz.
  sections
Roasted Salsa (see below)
Mexican Rub (see below)
1 avocado, peeled, seed removed, and sliced
Lime wedges
Cilantro

Roasted Salsa Ingredients

5 Roma tomatoes
2 tomatillos
1 jalapeño
1/2 onion
1 bulb garlic
2 tbsp Olive oil
Cilantro
1/2 lime
Sea salt
Coarse black pepper

Mexican Rub Ingredients

1 tsp paprika
1 tsp brown sugar
1 tsp sea salt
1/2 tsp ground chipotle powder
1/2 tsp coarse black pepper
1/4 tsp ground allspice

Roasted Salsa Instructions

1. Prepare the grill for the two-zone set up.
2. Prepare the Roasted Salsa: roast the tomatoes, tomatillos, jalapeño, and onion on the grill, on direct heat, until they are blistered and mostly blackened.
3. Slice off the top of the garlic bulb to expose the cloves, wrap the garlic in a loose sheet of foil with olive oil, and place it on the grill, on direct heat, until soft. Cover the grill with the lid and open the vents all the way.
4. When the roasted veggies are cooled down, place them all in a food processor or blender.
5. Squeeze the softened cloves of the garlic bulb into the processor/blender (adding some of the charred garlic skin is very tasty). Blend all ingredients well.
6. Add cilantro and squeeze lime juice into the processor, and blend for a few seconds.
7. Salt and pepper to taste.

Instructions

1. Mix together all rub ingredients in a small bowl.
2. Apply rub to flesh of the salmon.
3. Prepare the grill for the two-zone setup.

4.   Place the salmon, skin down, on the cool side of the grill. Cook for 4 to 6 minutes with the lid on and vents wide open.

5.   Take off the lid and grill the salmon flesh side down over direct heat until done (about 1 or 2 minutes).

6.   Remove from grill and serve immediately. Top salmon with Roasted Salsa, and garnish with avocados, lime, and cilantro.

SANIBEL BLACKENED SALMON

Serves: 4
Total Time: 20 minutes

I met Annie Swartz in Florida while on vacation. She is the seafood manager at a grocery store in Sanibel. I asked her if they had any blackening seasoning in the store and she enthusiastically gave me a paper with her own recipe. I promptly requested to use the recipe in this book and she was more than happy to contribute. I couldn't wait to get back home to try it. Simply amazing. Thanks Annie!

Ingredients
1 1/2 pounds wild Alaskan salmon, skin on
Annie's Blackening Spice (see below)
Cooking spray
1/2 cup Maggi Sweet Chili Sauce

Annie's Blackening Spice Ingredients
3/8 cup sweet paprika
1/4 cup salt
2 tbsp onion powder
2 tbsp garlic powder
2 tbsp cayenne pepper
1 tbsp white pepper
1 tbsp black pepper
1 tbsp dried thyme
1 tbsp dried oregano

Instructions
1. Prepare the blackening spice: combine all ingredients in a bowl and mix well.
2. Set up cooker for direct heat grilling at high heat.
3. Place a large cast-iron skillet directly over the heat source and get it really hot.
4. Cut the salmon into 6 oz. steaks. Coat the flesh of the salmon liberally with the seasoning.
5. Hit the skillet with cooking spray. You should see the pan smoke right away.
6. Add the salmon to the skillet, flesh side down, you want lots of smoke coming from the pan. Cook for 2 minutes.
7. When the salmon easily releases from the skillet, take the salmon out of the pan and move to the cool side of the grill to cook indirectly (with the lid on) for 8 minutes, skin side down.
8. Remove from the grill when the salmon reaches 140 degrees F internal temperature.
9. Brush on the sweet chili sauce.
10. Serve immediately.

CITRUS GOLDEN TROUT

Serves: 2
Total Time: 35 minutes

Ingredients

3 tbsp unsalted butter
1 tbsp roasted garlic
2 golden trout, cleaned and deboned with skin
    on
Canola oil
Kosher salt
Black pepper
1 tbsp fresh dill, rough chop
1 navel orange, sliced

Sauce

2 tbsp mayonnaise
1 tsp orange zest
2 tbsp orange juice
1 tsp fresh dill, chopped

Instructions

1.   Setup cooker for indirect heat at 375 degrees F.

2.   Combine sauce ingredients in a bowl and mix well, then refrigerate.

3.   In a small saucepan, melt butter on medium low heat and add garlic. Set aside.

4.   Open the trout cavity to expose the flesh, apply oil, and season with salt and pepper.

5.   Sprinkle the dill evenly over the trout and place the orange slices on top.

6.   Place the trout, skin side down, on the cool side of the grate and close the cook chamber.

7.   Cook for 10 minutes and baste with garlic butter.

8.   After another 10 minutes, check for doneness and remove from grill. (Cook longer if necessary.)

9.   Drizzle sauce over the trout and serve immediately.

GRILLED SHRIMP BOAT APPETIZER

Jason Szachnieski

Serves: 2
Total Time: 15 minutes

Ingredients

12 x 24-inch sheet of aluminum foil
1/2 pound of 31–40 count shrimp, raw, peeled,
  and deveined
1 tbsp Old Bay seasoning
4 tsp butter, divided into small pieces

Instructions

1. Create a "boat" by using a piece of 12 x 24-inch foil. Double the foil over to make a 12 x 12-inch piece and then fold up all 4 sides approximately 2 inches. Make sure to fold the corners so they will not leak while cooking.

2. Place shrimp evenly distributed in boat, season evenly with Old Bay seasoning, and add butter.

3. Place boat directly on grill.

4. Grill over hot coals for 7 minutes or until shrimp are cooked.

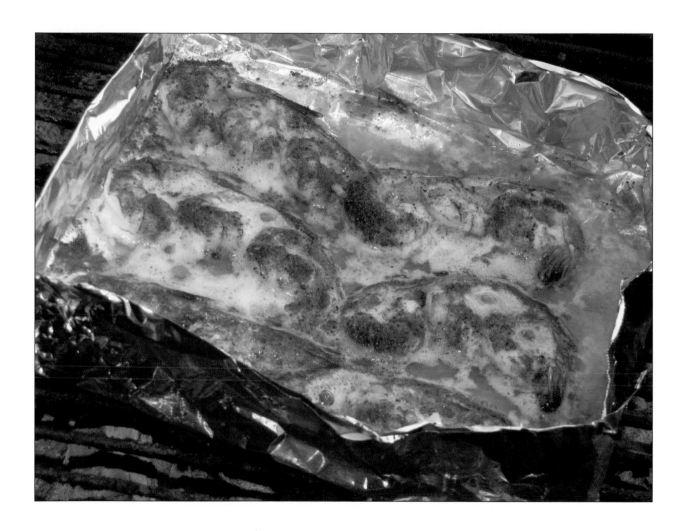

OYSTERS MEXIFELLER

Serves: 6
Total Time: 40 minutes

Ingredients

2 tbsp unsalted butter

1/4 cup red onion

2 oz. tequila

1/2 cup heavy cream

1 cup arugula, packed

2 tbsp cilantro, chopped

2 tbsp green onion, chopped

1/8 cup cotija cheese

6 oysters, shucked

1/2 cup corn chips, crushed

Salt and pepper, to taste

Instructions

1. Melt butter in pan over medium heat.

2. Add red onion.

3. Add tequila; wait 10 to 15 seconds.

4. Add heavy cream, bring to boil, and reduce slightly.

5. Add salt, pepper, arugula, cilantro, and green onion. Reduce until sauce thickens.

6. Add cotija and stir.

7. Remove pan from burner and let cool.

8. Spoon 1 tbsp of sauce into each oyster, top with corn chips, and cook on the grill for 10 minutes at 425 degrees F.

9. Remove from grill and serve.

Notes:

1. Try not to spill any of the oyster juice, that is most of the flavor!

2. To balance the oyster on the grill so it doesn't spill, take a sheet of aluminum foil and shape it into a ring to use it as a shell holder.

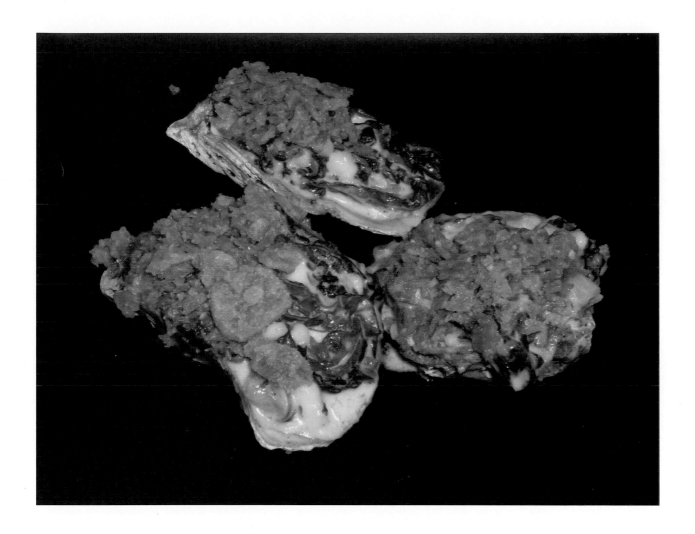

CHAPTER 9
OTHER RECIPES

ARTHUR'S CHILI

Serves: 5
Total Time: 3 hours

Got some leftovers? Or did you ruin a recipe? Make chili! I love to make this when I have excess brisket, especially burnt ends.

Ingredients

1 pound ground chuck, 80/20

1 pound smoked brisket, diced

4 cloves garlic, minced

1 medium yellow onion, diced

1 jalapeño, chopped

6 tbsp chili powder

2 tbsp cumin

1 28 oz. can diced tomatoes with juice

4 tsp Kosher salt

6 oz. dark beer

2 16 oz. cans chili beans

1 28 oz. jar pasta sauce

Instructions

1.   Brown the meat with garlic, onion, and jalapeños in skillet. Add 2 tbsp chili powder and 1 tbsp cumin.

2.   In a blender, add tomatoes, remaining chili powder and cumin, salt, and beer and blend well.

3.   Combine meat and sauce in a chili pot on medium heat and cook for 30 minutes.

4.   Add beans and pasta sauce.

5.   Simmer on low heat for 2 hours.

6.   For best results, refrigerate overnight, reheat, and serve.

KEY LIME CHEESECAKE

Serves: 12

Total Time: 2 hours + refrigeration time

Strawberry Coulis Ingredients

2 cups fresh strawberries

Zest of 1 lime

1–2 tablespoons sugar

Crust Ingredients

1 3/4 cups graham cracker crumbs
(about 12 whole graham crackers)

1/4 cup sugar

1/2 cup (1 stick) unsalted butter, melted

Filling Ingredients

3 8 oz. packages cream cheese, room
temperature

1/2 cup sour cream

1 cup sugar

5 large eggs

3 tablespoons fresh Key lime juice

2 teaspoons finely grated Key lime peel

3/4 teaspoon vanilla extract

Strawberry Coulis Instructions

1. Place 1 1/2 cups strawberries in a saucepan and add the lime zest. Mash with a fork and add 1 tablespoon sugar, stirring until dissolved.

2. Cook on the stove at medium heat. When the strawberries are just beginning to simmer, pour through a sieve into a bowl, pushing the berries with a large spoon to release the juice. Taste, adding more sugar if needed.

3. Refrigerate until ready to use.

Crust Instructions

1. Preheat grill to 350 degrees F. Butter a cake pan.

2. Stir graham cracker crumbs and sugar to blend in medium bowl.

3. Mix in butter until moistened. Press crumb mixture evenly onto bottom and 1 inch up sides of prepared pan.

4. Bake until set, about 5 minutes. Cool completely. Maintain grill temperature.

Filling Instructions

1. Using electric mixer, beat cream cheese in large bowl until smooth.

2. Beat in sour cream, then sugar. Beat in eggs 1 at a time, occasionally scraping down sides of bowl.

3. Beat in lime juice, lime peel, and vanilla.

4. Pour batter over prepared crust. Cover cheesecake pan loosely with foil.

5. Place cheesecake on grill. Bake 1 hour at 350 degrees F.

6. Uncover and continue to bake until just set in center when cake pan is gently shaken, about 20 minutes longer.

7. Remove and place directly into refrigerator; chill uncovered overnight.

8. Remove and serve topped with Strawberry Coulis.

SPICY PICKLES

Serves: 20
Total Cook Time: 20 minutes

Ingredients

1 tbsp pickling spice

1 1/2 tbsp Kosher salt

3 tbsp turbinado sugar

2 jalapeños, sliced

2 cloves garlic, crushed

1 tsp dill, chopped

1 1/2 cups boiling water

5 English cucumbers, sliced

1 cup white wine vinegar

Instructions

1.   In a large (1-quart) glass jar with a lid, combine pickling spice, salt, sugar, jalapeños, garlic, and dill.

2.   Pour boiling water into the jar and then add the cucumbers.

3.   Add the vinegar until the jar is full.

4.   Tightly screw lid on the jar, shake, and store in the refrigerator for 24 hours.

ROASTED BUTTERNUT SQUASH PANCAKES

Serves: 9
Total Time: 1 1/2 hours

Ingredients

1 butternut squash
Canola oil cooking spray
2 cups all purpose flour
2 tbsp sugar
2 tsp baking powder
1/2 tsp baking soda
3/4 tsp cinnamon
1/8 tsp nutmeg
1/2 tsp salt
1 1/4 cup milk
1/4 tsp cider vinegar
2 eggs
1/2 tsp vanilla

Instructions

1. Cut the butternut squash lengthwise. Wrap both halves in plastic wrap and cook in the microwave for 8 minutes.

2. Set up the two-zone method on the grill.

3. When the squash is cooled, unwrap the plastic and coat the flesh of the squash with cooking spray.

4. Place squash on grill using direct heat with the lid on, vents wide open.

5. Cook until tender or about 45 minutes.

6. Scoop out 3/4 cup cooked butternut squash and place it in a large bowl. Add all remaining ingredients and mix well.

7. Use a ladle to pour batter onto a cast-iron skillet on medium-low heat.

8. Cook the pancakes for 3 minutes on each side.

9. Serve immediately.

PARMESAN ONION RINGS

Serves: 4
Total Time: 1 hour

Ingredients
Canola oil
1 cup flour
2 eggs, beaten
2 cups panko breading
1/4 cup Parmesan cheese
2 tbsp Italian seasoning
1 large yellow onion, sliced

Dipping Sauce Ingredients
1/2 cup mayonnaise
1/3 cup ketchup
2 tbsp white vinegar
1 oz. Vidalia onions, chopped
2 tsp lemon juice
1 tsp Frank's Red Hot
1 tsp white sugar
1/2 tsp horseradish, grated
1/4 tsp Kosher salt
1/8 tsp Cayenne pepper

Instructions

1.   Prepare dipping sauce: combine all ingredients in a food processor and blend until smooth. Refrigerate until ready to use.

2.   Set up the cooker for direct heat grilling on high heat.

3.   Place a cast-iron skillet directly over the fire and fill the skillet with oil, about 1/8 inch deep.

4.   Place flour, eggs, and panko into 3 separate bowls. Add the cheese and Italian seasoning to the panko and mix well.

5.   Dredge each onion ring first in the flour, then the egg wash, and the panko mix last. Cook in the oil until the panko breading turns golden brown. Repeat the steps until all the rings are cooked. Replenish ingredients as necessary.

6.   Place the onion rings on a paper towel to let the oil drain from the rings.

7.   Serve the rings with the dipping sauce.

PROSPERITY SANDWICH

Serves: 2
Total Time: 45 minutes

Yet another St. Louis classic dish kicked up with smoked meats. I like my open-faced sandwich with a piece of thick cut bread from a loaf. One of these is more than enough to fill up on—this is definitely a rich man-sized sandwich.

Ingredients

2 tbsp unsalted butter

4 oz. mushrooms, sliced

1 shallot, chopped

2 slices bread, toasted

1/4 pound smoked turkey breast, sliced

1/2 pound smoked ham, sliced

4 slices tomato

2 slices bacon

Sauce

1 cup heavy cream

1 tbsp Dijon mustard

1/2 tsp Worcestershire sauce

1/2 cup nacho cheese

Black pepper, to taste

Instructions

1. In a saucepan, melt butter on medium heat. Sauté mushrooms and shallots.

2. Pour sautéed mix into a bowl and set aside.

3. Make the sauce. Combine all ingredients in saucepan on medium-low heat. Stir, reduce slightly, and let cool.

4. Evenly spread sautéed mix on toasted bread.

5. Top each slice of toast with slices of turkey and slices of ham.

6. Add tomato slices and pour the sauce over the sandwiches.

7. Use the broiler to melt the cheese sauce for a minute or so.

8. Top each sandwich with a slice of bacon and serve immediately.

OZARK SANDWICH

Serves: 1
Total Time: 20 minutes

I got fed up with the meager sliced bologna that came out of the plastic yellow and red packaging. My butcher was happy to cut man-sized bologna, which I promptly threw on my smoker and rubbed down with some spices. Chips in the sandwich are a must!

Ingredients

1 slice bologna, thick sliced
1 tsp BBQ Rub (page 330)
1 slice Swiss cheese
2 slices Texas Toast bread
2 tbsp mayonnaise
1 tsp Frank's Red Hot
Spicy Pickles (page 306)
1 oz. Doritos

Instructions

1. Set up the cooker for indirect heat grilling at 350 degrees F.

2. Lightly apply rub on both sides of bologna.

3. Place the bologna on the cool side of the grill to cook for 10 minutes.

4. Move the bologna to the direct heat and cook it directly over the fire to char up both sides.

5. Remove bologna from the fire and place the cheese on top.

6. Toast the bread and mix the mayo and hot sauce together. Spread the sauce on both slices of toast.

7. Place the bologna on 1 toast, top it with pickles and Doritos, and add another slice of toast.

8. Serve immediately.

GRAN PAPPY'S SMOKED APPLE CHEESECAKE

Tell You What BBQ (Steven Marx)
Competition BBQ Team (Sloatsburg, NY)
www.tellyouwhatbbq.com

Serves: 12
Total Time: 1 hour

Ingredients

2 cups all-purpose flour
1/2 cup firmly packed brown sugar
1 cup (2 sticks) butter, softened
2 8 oz. packages cream cheese, softened
1/2 cup sugar, plus 2 tbsp
2 large eggs
1 tsp vanilla extract
4 apples, peeled, cored, and sliced to form rings
    (Paula Reds or Granny Smith work well)
1/2 tsp ground cinnamon
1/4 tsp ground nutmeg

Finishing Sauce

1 tbsp butter
Cinnamon sugar (1/4 cup white sugar mixed
    with 1 1/2 tbsp cinnamon)
2 tbsp maple syrup
Whipped Topping
1 cup heavy cream

1/4 cup sugar
1 teaspoon vanilla

Whipped topping instructions

1.   In a large chilled metal mixing bowl, pour the heavy cream in the bowl and use a stand mixer or hand mixer and start mixing on High.

2.   When the cream achieves soft peaks, slowly add the sugar and vanilla while mixing.

3.   Mix until the whipped cream has stiff peaks.

4.   Keep refrigerated until ready to use.

Instructions

1.   Preheat grill for indirect cooking at 350 degrees F. Do not add smoke wood.

2.   In a large, pre-chilled stainless bowl, combine flour and brown sugar. Cut in butter with a pastry blender until mixture is crumbly. Press evenly into a 13 x 9 x 2-inch baking pan lined with heavy-duty aluminum foil. Bake on the grill approximately 15 minutes or until lightly browned.

3.   In a fairly large bowl, beat cream cheese with 1/2 cup sugar using an electric mixer at medium speed until smooth. Then add eggs, 1 at a time, and vanilla. Stir to combine. Pour over warm crust.

4.   Combine slices from 3 apples (reserving 4 slices for the finishing sauce), remaining 2 tablespoons sugar, cinnamon, and nutmeg.

Spoon evenly over cream cheese mixture. Bake 30 minutes on the grill, or until filling is set. You will see it firm up. Remove from grill. Let cool for at least an hour (refrigerate if possible). Do not cut yet.

5. Now the flip! Place a flat tray on top of cheesecake pan.

6. Flip over the tray and cheesecake together and place on counter. Peel foil off bottom of cheesecake and flip again to upright. Slice and plate the cheesecake.

7. For the finishing sauce, in a saucepan heat butter and cinnamon sugar. Place the remaining apple slices flat in pan. Heat both sides of apple, add maple syrup, and heat until warm.

8. Pour the sweetened apples over the cheesecake and top with a dollop of whipped cream.

9. Try not to eat all of the dessert!

GRILLED PEACHES AND ICE CREAM

Serves: 4
Total Time: 15 minutes

A longtime favorite summer treat in my family. I knew one day this would make it into a cookbook!

Ingredients

4 peaches
4 tbsp butter
1/3 cup brown sugar
1/4 dark rum
1/2 tsp ground cinnamon
1/2 tsp nutmeg
1/4 tsp salt
Vanilla ice cream

Instructions

1. Slice peaches in half and discard pits.

2. Set up the grill for direct heat cooking on high heat.

3. Combine butter, brown sugar, rum, cinnamon, nutmeg, and salt in a foil pan. Place pan on the heated grill.

4. After the butter melts, mix ingredients until well blended. Add peaches flesh down in the pan.

5. After 5 minutes, place peaches directly on the grill, flesh down.

6. After a few minutes, turn peaches over and brush the rum sauce over them.

7. Peaches are done when they are very soft. Place peaches back in foil pan and remove from the grill.

8. Serve peaches with ice cream, drizzling excess rum sauce over peaches.

FRENCH TOAST WITH PECAN GLAZE

Serves: 6–8
Total Time: 1 hour

Ingredients

1 loaf challah bread
8 eggs
1 1/2 cups half & half
1 cup milk
2 tbsp sugar
1 tsp vanilla extract
1/4 tsp cinnamon
1/4 tsp nutmeg
Salt to taste
Maple syrup, to serve

Pecan Crust

1 stick butter
1 cup light brown sugar
1 cup pecans, chopped
2 tbsp light corn syrup
1/2 tsp cinnamon
1/2 tsp nutmeg

Instructions

1.   Slice challah bread into 1-inch slices and layer in a buttered 9x13-inch baking dish in rows.

2.   In a large mixing bowl, combine eggs, half & half, milk, sugar, vanilla, cinnamon, nutmeg, and salt and beat with a whisk until fully blended.

3.   Pour mixture over bread slices, covering each piece.

4.   Cover with foil and refrigerate overnight.

5.   Preheat oven to 350 degrees F. Meanwhile, combine all ingredients for Pecan Crust together and spread over casserole.

6.   Bake for 40 minutes and serve immediately with maple syrup.

CRISPY VIDALIA ONIONS

Serves: 2
Total Time: 10 minutes

Ingredients

2 cups canola oil
1/2 medium Vidalia onion

Instructions

1.   Pour oil into a saucepan and heat at medium-high heat.

2.   Cut the onion into rings and fry them in the oil until they caramelize and develop a crispy texture.

3.   Cool the cooked onions on paper towels.

Notes:

1.   Substitute yellow, white, green, or red onions for this recipe.

2.   Use the onion-flavored oil to make into a dressing or a dipping sauce.

CHICHARONES

Serves: 4
Total Time: 45 minutes

I can't get enough of this salty pork-flavored goodness. If you were bold enough to give the lengua a try (page 216), then this is right up your cornhole!

Ingredients
1 pound fresh pig skin
Kosher salt

Instructions

1.   A good piece of pig skin has about an inch of fat with meat still attached to the skin. Do not worry about the hair—it will cook off.

2.   Square up the skin and cut into 1-inch cubes. Save or discard the excess skin.

3.   Set up the cooker for indirect heat cooking at 350 degrees F.

4.   In a foil pan with a cooling rack inside, place the chunks skin side down on the rack. Season the chunks with salt. Cover and seal the pan with a sheet of aluminum foil. Place the foil pan directly over the fire and keep the lid on the cooker. Cook for 15 minutes.

5.   Cook for another 20 minutes on the cool side of the grill.

6.   Remove the chicharones from the grill and remove the foil. The chicharones should look golden brown and crispy.

7.   Serve immediately. They will melt in your mouth if eaten right after cooking. They will turn a little tough and chewy after some time, but the flavor gets better.

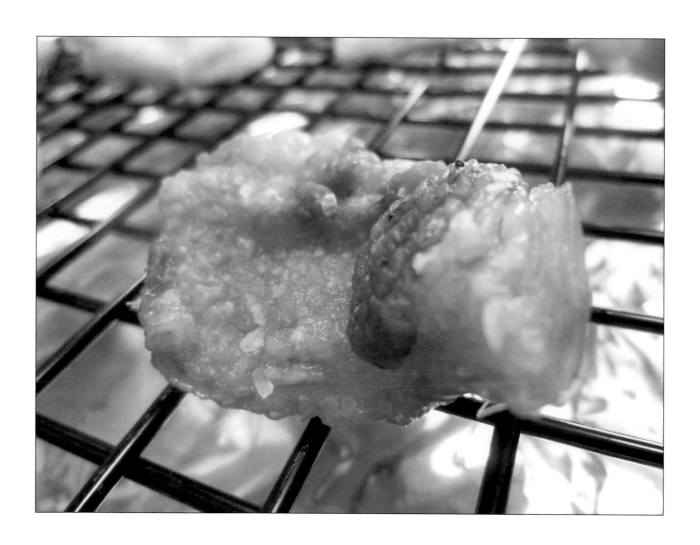

BROWNIE TRIFLE

Jamie Aguirre

Serves: 6
Total Time: 4 hours, 35 minutes

Ingredients

1 box brownie mix (1 pound, 2.3 oz.), prepared as
    directed
1 box chocolate pudding mix (4-serving size),
    prepared as directed
1 bag of Heath Toffee Bits
1 container of whipped cream or whipped
    topping
1 chocolate bar
3 cream-filled rolled wafers (such as Pepperidge
    Farm Pirouette Rolled Wafers)

Instructions

1. Heat grill to 350 degrees F.
2. Grease bottom of aluminum foil pan with cooking spray (do not use butter or oil as it can stick or burn to the bottom of the pan).
3. Make brownie mix as directed on box and pour evenly into foil pan.
4. Cover foil pan with aluminum foil to avoid ashes getting into mix and place on the grill.
5. Check frequently, but cook as directed on box. Since this is being cooked on the grill, the cooking time varies every time. To test for doneness, use a toothpick. If you put in a toothpick and it comes out clean, it is time to pull them.
6. While brownies are cooking, make pudding and refrigerate until you are ready to use.
7. Cut brownies into squares and place into 6 individual trifle dishes.
8. Add a scoop of pudding over each brownie.
9. Top with a generous sprinkling of toffee bits and a scoop of whipped cream.
10. Using a potato peeler, peel slices of chocolate off of the chocolate bar over the top of the whipped cream.
11. Follow same procedure on each trifle.
12. Cover and refrigerate for at least 4 hours before serving.
13. Add half a wafer to each trifle.
14. Serve and enjoy!

CHAPTER 10
RUBS, SAUCES, & MORE

ALL PURPOSE GRILLING RUB

Ingredients
1 tbsp Kosher salt
1/2 tbsp pepper
1 tsp garlic salt
1/2 tsp crushed red pepper flakes

Instructions
Combine all ingredients in a bowl and mix well.

MLG BBQ Rub
Ingredients
1/2 cup turbinado sugar
3 tbsp Kosher salt
1 tbsp garlic powder
1 tbsp onion powder
1 tbsp chili powder
1 tbsp Hungarian paprika
1 tbsp black pepper
1/2 tsp cayenne pepper

Instructions
Combine all ingredients in a bowl and mix well.

MLG Poultry Rub
Ingredients
1 tbsp garlic salt
1 tbsp onion powder
1/2 tbsp chili powder
1/2 tbsp paprika
1/4 tbsp black pepper

Instructions
Combine all ingredients in a bowl and mix well.

Mexican Rub
Ingredients
1 tsp coarse black pepper
1 tsp sea salt
1 tsp ground Mexican oregano
1 tsp minced dried onion
1 tsp minced dried garlic

Instructions
Combine all ingredients in a bowl and mix well.

MLG Pollo Rub
Ingredients
1 tsp garlic salt
1 tsp chili powder
1/2 tsp white pepper
1/4 tsp thyme, ground
1/4 tsp marjoram, ground

Instructions
Combine all ingredients in a bowl and mix well.

Fiesta #1 Rub
Ingredients
4 tbsp cumin
4 tbsp oregano
1 tsp jalapeño powder

1 tsp smoked paprika

1 tsp white pepper

1 tsp black pepper

1 tsp salt

Instructions

Combine all ingredients in a bowl and mix well.

Fiesta #2 Rub

Ingredients

2 tbsp Hungarian paprika

1 tsp ground green jalapeño pepper

1 tsp ground white pepper

1 tbsp dark roasted chili powder

1/2 tsp Worcestershire powder

1 tbsp oregano

1 tbsp ground cumin

1/2 tsp ground cinnamon

1 tsp granulated garlic

1 tsp Kosher salt

Instructions

Combine all ingredients in a bowl
and mix well.

Apple Rub

Ingredients

2 tbsp brown sugar

1 tbsp Hungarian paprika

1 tsp apple pie spice

1/2 tsp garlic powder

1/2 tsp onion powder

1/2 tsp black pepper

1/2 tsp Kosher salt

Instructions

Combine all ingredients in a bowl and mix well.

Beef Rub

Ingredients

1 tbsp garlic salt

1 tbsp pepper

1 tsp Hungarian paprika

1 tsp accent seasoning

1/2 tbsp onion powder

1/2 tbsp white sugar

1/4 tsp fennel, ground

1/4 tsp celery, ground

1/4 tsp chile de arbol

Instructions

Combine all ingredients in a bowl
and mix well.

Annie's Blackening Spice

Annie Swartz

Ingredients

3/8 cup sweet paprika

1/4 cup salt

2 tbsp onion powder

2 tbsp garlic powder

2 tbsp cayenne pepper

1 1/2 tbsp white pepper

1 1/2 tbsp black pepper

1 tbsp dried thyme

1 tbsp dried oregano

Instructions

1. In a medium bowl, combine all ingredients and mix well.
2. Store in a sealable jar at room temperature.
3. Good for 6 months.
4. Use on seafood, poultry, and pork.

Jeff's St. Louis-Style Rub
Ingredients

1 cup brown sugar

1 cup white sugar

1/3 cup celery salt

1/3 cup black pepper

1/3 cup garlic powder

1/3 cup dry mustard

1/3 cup onion powder

1 tbsp cayenne pepper

Instructions

Combine all ingredients in a bowl and mix well.

Cole's Basic Rib Rub
Ingredients

1/2 cup dark brown sugar

1/4 cup paprika

1/8 cup salt

1 tbsp black pepper

2 tbsp hot chili powder

1 tbsp garlic powder

1 tbsp onion powder

1 tsp cayenne pepper

1 tsp cinnamon

Instructions

Combine all ingredients in a bowl and mix well.

Grillin' Fools Rub
Ingredients

2 tbsp granulated garlic

2 tbsp turbinado sugar (raw sugar)

2 tbsp pumpkin pie spice

1 tbsp sweet paprika

Instructions

Combine all ingredients in a bowl and mix well.

Slabs A' Smokin Basic Chicken Rub
Ingredients

2 tbsp sea salt

1 1/2 tbsp granulated garlic

1 tbsp granulated onion

1 tsp ground thyme

1 1/2 tsp paprika

1 tsp black pepper

1/2 tsp dry mustard

Instructions

Combine all ingredients in a small bowl.

MLG Barbecue Sauce
Ingredients

1/2 cup unsalted butter

3 cloves garlic, minced

1/2 small yellow onion, chopped

1/2 green pepper, chopped

1/4 cup bourbon

1/2 cup dark brown sugar

1/2 cup light corn syrup

2 cups ketchup

2 cups water

1 tbsp unsulfured blackstrap molasses

1/4 cup apple cider vinegar

2 tsp Kosher salt

1 tbsp red pepper flakes

1/2 tbsp black pepper

Instructions

1.   In a saucepan on medium heat, melt the butter and add garlic, onions, and green peppers. Cook until they are soft.

2.   Add the remaining ingredients and mix well.

3.   Let the sauce simmer and slightly thicken for about 10 minutes.

4.   Remove from the heat and let it cool.

5.   Pour the sauce into a food processor and blend until smooth.

6.   Use immediately or store in a jar with a lid and refrigerate.

Hot Cinnamon BBQ Sauce
Ingredients

1/4 cup orange juice

1/2 cup Red Hots candy

1 cup ketchup

3 tbsp Worcestershire sauce

2 tbsp molasses

2 tsp Granny Smith apples, finely minced

1 tsp garlic, finely minced

1/2 tsp Hungarian paprika

1/4 tsp red pepper flakes

Instructions

1.   In a saucepan on medium heat, combine the orange juice and candy. Put the lid on and cook until the candy is melted down.

2.   Add remaining ingredients into the saucepan, then mix well and reduce the heat to a simmer for 15 minutes. Sauce is done when it thickens.

3.   Let the sauce cool and store it in a glass jar, refrigerated, until ready to use.

Ginger Honey Glaze
Ingredients

1/2 cup honey

1/2 stick unsalted butter

1/4 cup ginger ale

2 tbsp cider vinegar

1 tsp red pepper flakes

1/2 tsp minced garlic

1/2 tsp Worcestershire sauce

Instructions

1.   Heat all ingredients in a small saucepan and mix well.

2.   Ready to use when cool.

Grillin' Fools Glaze
Ingredients

2 tbsp apple jelly

2 tbsp apricot preserves

2 tbsp hot pepper jelly

2 tsp Worcestershire sauce

Instructions

1. Combine the glaze ingredients in a bowl and microwave for about 90 seconds to liquefy the gelatin and allow the ingredients to combine.

2. Mix well.

South Carolina Mustard Sauce
Ingredients

1/2 cup prepared yellow mustard

1/4 cup apple cider vinegar

5 tbsp dark brown sugar

1/2 tsp paprika

1/2 tsp Worcestershire sauce

1/2 tsp white pepper

1/2 tsp cayenne pepper

1/4 tsp black pepper

Instructions

1. Combine all ingredients in a medium saucepan on medium heat.

2. Stir until all ingredients are dissolved and mixed well.

3. Serve when sauce has cooled.

Claudia's BBQ Sauce
Ingredients

3/4 of a 40 oz. bottle of Sweet Baby Ray's BBQ Sauce

2 tbsp apple cider vinegar

1/3 cup pineapple juice

1/8 tsp ground ginger

1 tsp tequila

Instructions

1. Combine all ingredients in a medium saucepan on medium heat.

2. Stir until all ingredients are dissolved and mixed well.

3. Serve when sauce has cooled.

NON-BARBECUE SAUCES

Red Chile Sauce
Ingredients
12 dried peppers (8 pasilla, 4 ancho)
5 cups water
1/2 medium yellow onion
1 bulb garlic
1 tbsp cilantro, chopped
1 vegetable bouillon cube
Salt and pepper, to taste

Instructions
1. Roast the dried peppers; do not burn. Soak them in water until soft.
2. Roast onion and garlic.
3. Drain the chiles, reserving 1 cup of the soaking water.
4. Combine chile water, peppers, onion, and garlic in a food processor and puree until smooth.
5. Add cilantro, bouillon cube and salt and pepper to chile sauce, and puree again until it is salsa consistency (adding more water if necessary).
6. With a fine mesh strainer, separate the liquids from the solids.
7. The solids left in the strainer are chile paste, and the chile liquid can be used as a red sauce for burritos, enchiladas, huevos rancheros, etc.
8. Store each of the items in a glass container and refrigerate to keep fresh.

Bistro Sauce
Ingredients
2 tbsp mayonnaise
2 tbsp Andria's Steak Sauce (or any gourmet steak sauce)

Instructions
Combine ingredients and mix well. Refrigerate until ready to use.

Tzatziki Sauce
Ingredients
3 tbsp olive oil
1 tbsp apple cider vinegar
2 cloves garlic, minced finely
1/2 tsp salt
1/4 tsp white pepper
1 shallot, chopped
1/4 tsp cayenne pepper
1 tsp pepper sauce
1 tbsp Greek seasoning
1 cup Greek yogurt, strained
1 cup sour cream
1 cucumber, peeled, seeded, and diced
1 tsp chopped fresh dill

Instructions
1. Combine olive oil, vinegar, garlic, salt, pepper, shallot, cayenne pepper, pepper sauce,

and Greek seasoning in a food processor. Mix until well combined.

2.   Using a whisk, blend the yogurt with the sour cream.

3.   Add the olive oil mixture to the yogurt mixture and mix well.

4.   Add the cucumber and chopped fresh dill.

5.   Chill for at least 2 hours before serving.

6.   Garnish with a sprig of fresh dill just before serving.

Chipotle Sauce
Ingredients
4 Roma tomatoes

1/2 medium onion

3 cloves garlic

1 tbsp chopped cilantro

2 cups chicken broth

2 chipotle peppers (from a can)

1/2 cup adobo sauce

Instructions
1.   Setup the two-zone grill method.

2.   Roast the tomatoes and onion until you see some grill marks.

3.   Put the tomatoes, onion, and all remaining ingredients in a food processor and blend well. Don't puree—leave it a little chunky.

4.   Pour the sauce into a 9 x 12-inch aluminum foil pan.

5.   Store sauce in the fridge until ready to use.

Horseradish Sauce
Ingredients
1 oz. fresh horseradish, grated

1/3 cup mayonnaise

1 tbsp sour cream

1/4 tsp Dijon mustard

2 drops Worcestershire sauce

Salt and pepper, to taste

Instructions
Mix all ingredients for horseradish the day before using. Keep in fridge.

Chimichurri Sauce
Ingredients
4 cloves garlic

2 tbsp yellow onions, chopped

1 cup fresh flat leaf parsley

1 cup fresh cilantro

1/4 cup fresh oregano leaves

1/2 cup olive oil

1 tbsp lime juice, freshly squeezed

2 tbsp red wine vinegar

2 tbsp Kosher salt

2 tbsp crushed red pepper flakes

Instructions
1.   In a food processor (or blender), pulse the garlic and onion until finely chopped.

2.   Add the parsley, cilantro, and oregano and pulse briefly, until finely chopped (not pureed).

3. Place the mixture in a bowl. Add the olive oil, lime juice, and vinegar, and mix well by hand.

4. Season with salt and red pepper flakes.

5. Store in the refrigerator until ready to serve.

Freakin' Good Mustard Sauce
Ingredients
1/4 cup mayonnaise

1/4 cup honey mustard

1/4 cup Woeber's Sweet n Hot Mustard

Instructions
Mix all ingredients together.

BRINES & INJECTIONS

Basic Brine 101
Ingredients

1 gallon ice water

1/2 cup Kosher salt

1/2 cup white sugar

Instructions

1. Pour 4 cups of the ice water into a large saucepan and bring to a boil.

2. Dissolve the salt and sugar in the boiling water, then turn off heat and let cool.

3. Pour the brine mixture into a 2-gallon storage bag, add the rest of the ice water, and mix well.

4. Brine is ready to use.

Pork Brine
Ingredients

8 cups ice cold water

1/2 cup Kosher salt

1/4 cup sugar

2 tbsp unsulfured molasses

1 tbsp red pepper flakes

1 tbsp dried thyme leaves

Instructions

1. Turn on stove to medium-high heat.

2. In a large saucepan, combine 2 cups of water with the salt and sugar.

3. Heat and stir continuously until the sugar and salt are dissolved. Take the brine off heat and let it cool.

4. Pour the remaining ingredients into a large container that has a lid.

5. Add the brine to the large container and mix well.

Cider Brine
Ingredients

2 cups apple juice

2 cups water

1/3 cup Kosher salt

1/3 cup brown sugar

2 tbsp red pepper flakes

1/2 tsp ground cinnamon

Instructions

1. In a saucepan, bring apple juice, water, salt, and brown sugar to a boil, stirring regularly.

2. When all is dissolved, take saucepan off heat and let the brine cool.

3. Pour the rest of the ingredients into a container that has a lid.

4. Add the brine to the large container and mix well.

Turkey Brine

1 gallon water, cold

1 cup Kosher salt

1 cup white sugar

1 oz. fresh herbs (thyme, rosemary, and sage)

2 bay leaves

1 lemon, halved

1 tbsp black peppercorns

5 cloves garlic, crushed

1 medium yellow onion, chopped

Instructions

1. In a saucepan, bring 5 cups of water to a boil. Dissolve the salt and sugar in the boiling water. Let the solution cool.
2. Add all the brine ingredients into a container and shake up the container to evenly distribute all the ingredients.

MLG Pollo Brine

4 cups water

1/2 cup Kosher salt

1/2 cup white sugar

4 sprigs thyme

1 lemon peel

1 shallot, chopped

1 tbsp garlic, minced

Instructions

1. In a saucepan, bring water, salt, and sugar to a boil, stirring regularly.

2. When all is dissolved, take saucepan off heat and let the brine cool.

3. Pour the rest of the ingredients into a container that has a lid.

4. Add the brine to the large container and mix well.

Grillin' Fools Ribs Brine
Ingredients

1 quart apple juice

1/4 cup table salt

2 tbsp minced garlic

1 tsp fresh cracked black pepper

Instructions

Combine everything in a storage bag and slosh around until the salt is dissolved.

Slabs A' Smokin Chicken Brine
Ingredients

1 cup water

1 cup apple juice

1 can of Sprite

1/2 cup Kosher or sea salt

1 tbsp pepper

Instructions

Combine ingredients in a storage bag and mix well until the salt is dissolved.

Basic Pork Injection
Ingredients

2 cups apple juice

2 tbsp BBQ Rub (page 330)

Instructions

1. Boil the ingredients in a saucepan until the rub dissolves. Let it cool.

2. Fill an injection needle and start injecting the liquid into the meat.

MLG Pork Injection
Ingredients
2 cups apple juice

1/4 cup pineapple juice

1/4 cup soy sauce

1 tbsp Worcestershire sauce

1 garlic bulb, roasted

1 tsp BBQ Rub (page 330)

1/4 cup Vidalia onion, diced

1/2 tsp Kosher salt

1/2 tsp black pepper

Instructions
1.   In a medium saucepan, combine all the ingredients and cook over medium heat.

2.   Stir mixture until the ingredients are mostly dissolved. Let it cool.

3.   Pour mixture into a food processor and mix until smooth.

4.   Use immediately or store in the refrigerator.

ASSORTED FOOD FARE

Pico de Gallo

2 Roma tomatoes, diced

1 jalapeño, deseeded, deveined, and diced

1/2 cup white onion, diced

1 tbsp cilantro, chopped

2 tbsp lime juice

1/2 tsp Kosher salt

Instructions

Combine all ingredients and mix well. Refrigerate until ready to use.

Pickled Red Onions

Ingredients

1/2 cup apple cider vinegar

1/2 cup water

1/2 cup sugar

1/2 tsp Kosher salt

1/2 red onion, sliced into thin rings

2 cloves garlic, crushed

Instructions

1. In a saucepan, bring apple cider vinegar, water, sugar, and salt to a boil, stirring occasionally. Take off the heat and let it cool.

2. In a container with a lid, add onion and garlic.

3. Pour the cooled liquid into the container and refrigerate until ready to use.

Beef Paste

Ingredients

1 tbsp beef base paste

1 tbsp chile paste (optional; see Red Chile Sauce, page 335)

1/2 tsp soy sauce

1/2 tsp Worcestershire sauce

Instructions

1. Mix all ingredients thoroughly.

2. Refrigerate for 30 minutes before using.

Jalapeño–Tomatillo Aioli

Ingredients

1 tomatillo, husked

1 jalapeño

2 cloves garlic

1/2 cup mayonnaise

1/2 tsp lemon juice, freshly squeezed

1/2 tsp Dijon mustard

Salt and pepper, to taste

Instructions

1. Roast tomatillo and jalapeño, by cooking over direct heat at 500+ degrees F on the grill. When the tomatillo and jalapeno are slightly charred, remove from the grill.

2. Remove stem and most seeds from jalapeño.

3. Combine all ingredients in food processor and blend until smooth.

4. Store in the refrigerator until ready to use.

Hot Bacon Dressing
Ingredients
1 tsp bacon grease

1 tbsp honey

1 tbsp grainy mustard

1 onion, chopped

1 tbsp apple cider vinegar

1/2 cup water

1 tsp Cornstarch and 2 tsp water, mixed into a
    paste

6 slices cooked bacon

Salt and pepper

Instructions
1.   In a saucepan, cook bacon grease, honey, mustard, onions, vinegar and water on medium heat until it begins to boil, add the cornstarch paste, and stir as the dressing starts to thicken.

2.   Remove from the heat and set aside at room temperature.

3.   Stir in the bacon and season with salt and pepper.

Onion Jam
Ingredients
2 medium onions, sliced

Large pinch of salt

Bacon fat

1 tbsp balsamic vinegar

2 tbsp dark brown sugar

Instructions
1.   Spread onions in a cast-iron skillet and sprinkle pinch of salt over onions.

2.   Cook onions in bacon fat over medium-low heat until soft, about 20 minutes.

3.   Spread balsamic vinegar and dark brown sugar over onions. Cook for another 10 minutes until thickened. Set aside.

Bacon Jam
Ingredients
2 pounds sliced maple bacon

1 large onion, sliced

2 shallots, sliced

4 cloves garlic, minced

4 tbsp Twisted Belly's BBQ Rub

1/2 cup dark rum

1/2 cup maple syrup

1/3 cup Twisted Belly's Melon Madness BBQ
    Sauce

1/4 cup white vinegar

1/4 cup cider vinegar

6 tbsp turbinado sugar

2 tbsp hot sauce

Instructions
1.   Preheat the smoker to about 275 to 300 degrees F and add 1 or 2 chunks of apple wood.

2.   Place all the bacon in the smoker with an aluminum pan below to catch the grease (you will need this later). Cook for about 45 minutes to 1 hour or until crisp.

3.   Use cast iron when possible, but any saucepan will work. Preheat a cast-iron Dutch oven over low to medium heat and add the grease from the bacon. If there is not enough grease, you can use vegetable oil.

4.   Once the grease or oil is preheated, add the onions and allow to soften for about 15 to 20 minutes or until translucent.

5.   Add the sliced shallots, minced garlic, and the BBQ Rub to the onions and cook for 2 to 3 minutes. (Do not let the garlic burn.)

6.   Add the remaining ingredients and mix. Make sure that all the sugar has dissolved completely.

7.   Allow this mixture to cook for 1 hour to thicken and reduce.

8.   Remove from the heat and allow to cool for another hour.

9.   Add the cooled mixture to your food processor along with the cooked bacon.

10. Mix all ingredients until the bacon is chopped and mixed evenly throughout. Do not over-mix.

11. With a spatula, remove mixture from the food processor and enjoy. This can be served cold or warm.

Acknowledgments, Contributors, and Product Listings

This cookbook is only as good as the people who are behind the content. Each one of these contributors is a reflection of the talent and passion folks have for barbecue. Whether we are preparing a catering service for a client, holding that SLR camera with a steady hand at a well-lighted plate of ribs, anxiously waiting for that first turn-in, or gearing up for that backyard Friday night grillfest—barbecue makes us happy and keeps us going.

Please help me acknowledge these contributors from across the country. Furthermore, don't forget to check out all these guys on Facebook and Twitter. Each pitmaster on this list brings his or her own unique style of barbecue and the enthusiasm to share it with everyone. The barbecue community is truly a tight-knit group that cherishes camaraderie and community service above all else. I'm proud to be associated with many individuals and organizations that willingly and unselfishly give back to their neighborhood through the activities of barbecue.

Thank you to all my cookbook buddies. I'm a fan of your websites and blogs, I love to use your products, I'm glad we met through barbecue and social media . . . and I'm still trying to kick all your butts in competition barbecue. I am forever indebted to you all for making great barbecue happen.

Finally, to my family, the best support system anybody could ask for. However, my wife Jamie deserves most of the credit. She's been taking care of me and raising our kids during the production of this cookbook. She has been responsible for my many barbecue accolades, inside and outside of competition. In competition, she is known as The General, and despite all the meat being prepared, cooked, presented, and eaten, she has never tasted my award-winning barbecue because she's vegetarian. That's love at its finest. I love you, Jamie.

Jamie Aguirre

Teresa Aguirre

B&B BBQ (Jeff Brinker)
Competition BBQ Team and Catering Company
www.brinkercatering4u.com

Canadian Bakin' (Al Bowman)
Competition BBQ Team

Cole's Sweet Heat (Cole Harte)
Competition BBQ Team and BBQ Sauce Company
www.colessweetheat.com

Code 3 Spices (Chris Bohnemeier)
BBQ Rub Company
www.code3spices.com

Extraordinary BBQ Blog (Kevin Haberberger)
Slabs A' Smokin Competition BBQ Team
www.extraordinarybbq.com

Juli Getzlaf

Getting Basted (Brad Leighninger)
Competition BBQ Team and BBQ Bloggers
www.gettinbasted.com

Grillin' Fools (Scott Thomas)
BBQ Blogger
www.grillinfools.com

Sharon Hohman

Chef Todd Kussman

Lock, Stock and Two Smokin' Barrels (Bill Grenko)
Competition BBQ Team
www.lsatsb.blogspot.ca

The Man, The Grill, The Magic (Don Parr)
Competition BBQ Team
www.donsgrilling.blogspot.com

Nibble Me This (Chris Grove)
BBQ Blogger
www.nibblemethis.com

Patio Daddio BBQ (John Dawson)
BBQ Blogger
www.patiodaddiobbq.com

Phatso's BBQ (Jeff Fitter)
Catering Company and Competition BBQ Team
www.phatsosbbq.com

Simpson BBQ (Daniel Simpson)
BBQ Blogger
www.simpsonbbq.com

Annie Swartz

Carl Swartz

Jason Szachnieski

Tell You What BBQ (Steven Marx)
Competition BBQ Team (Sloatsburg, NY)
Greg Casarella
Stephen Marx
Tim Mendolia
Dave McNally
Carmine Sgueglia
Mike Sullivan
John Callanan
www.tellyouwhatbbq.com

Twisted Belly (Fritz Wiesehan)
Competition BBQ Team

America's Top BBQ Competitions

1. American Royal (Invitational & Open) – Kansas City, MO

The American Royal Open is the world's largest BBQ competition with over 500 teams competing to be literally crowned Grand Champion. The American Royal is a three-day event with 2 championship contests and various ancillary categories that put the best pit masters against each other in this ultimate double blind judging throw down. The Invitational is a competition in which only Grand Champions from sanctioned regional contests can compete. In addition, Friday night is reserved for the largest barbecue party in America. Everyone and their mother converges on the area of the Kemper arena parking lot known as the "dark side" . . . it is epic!

2. The World Championship Barbecue Cooking Contest – Memphis, TN

Located right off the muddy banks of the Mississippi River, this Memphis in May event determines a World Champion in three pork categories (ribs, pork shoulder, and whole hog). Competitors are required to present their barbecue to judges in a personal setting for two rounds of judging and explain why their barbecue deserves to win. Winners of each category are given the opportunity to win Grand Champion with the highest overall score.

3. Jack Daniels Invitational – Lynchburg, TN

You must win in order to get an Invitation to this prestigious event. Even then, you're not guaranteed unless your bung is called . . . yes, a bung. Some of the most iconic masters of barbecue won this contest, but to win, you must incorporate the sour mash liquor into your barbecue recipe and be at the mercy of the judges.

4. World Food Championships – Las Vegas, NV

The new kid on the block in the championship barbecue circuit is the WFC. Big prize money draws in Grand Champions from around the world to compete tournament style at this cut throat event. Other culinary categories such as chili, burgers, and dessert are represented at this competition, but barbecue is the main attraction.

5. Sam's Club Invitational – Bentonville, AR

Before reaching the final round of this competition, only a limited number of teams can prove themselves in 25 local contests. The top 6 in each local contest move on to compete in 5 regional contests. The top 10 of each regional contest move on to the finals. A total cash prize of $500,000 is up for grabs and the honor of Tour Club champion cements your place in barbecue lore.

6. Kingsford Invitational – NYC in 2013

Another recent addition to the BBQ circuit, this event invites the biggest names in barbecue to cook against each other in a $50,000 winner take all competition. The Veterans Day weekend competition hosts the contest at different locations, so there is no telling where the next event will take place. That makes this contest the most unique of the bunch.